VIVAT HEATHROW!
AIRPORT LIFE UNWRAPPED

BY

PETER EDMUNDS

CIRRUS ASSOCIATES

PUBLISHED BY:
Cirrus Associates (S.W.),
Kington Magna,
Gillingham,
Dorset,
SP8 5EW UK.

All rights reserved. No part of this publication may be reproduced, stored in a retrieval system, or transmitted in any form or by any means, electronic, mechanical, photocopying or otherwise without the prior permission of the publisher.

© Peter Edmunds 2000

ISBN 1 902807 10 3

PRINTED IN ENGLAND BY:
The Book Factory,
35-37 Queensland Road,
London,
N7 7AH.

PHOTO SCANNING BY:
Castle Graphics Ltd.,
Nunney,
Nr. Frome,
Somerset,
BA11 4LW.

DISTRIBUTORS:
Cirrus Associates (S.W.),
Little Hintock,
Kington Magna,
Gillingham,
Dorset,
SP8 5EW.

COVER PHOTO: A night view of a BA Boeing 747 departing Terminal 3 (from the author's personal collection – possibly by Arthur Kemsley, BAA). INSIDE PHOTOS: All taken by the author or from his personal collection, which includes some photos by Arthur Kemsley, BAA.)

DEDICATION

To: Heathrow Travel Care,

the Airport Social Work Agency.

(See pages 120-125 for a description of the work of **Travel Care**.)

Every book sold will help to support **Travel Care** in caring for passengers, staff and public at Heathrow.

ACKNOWLEDGMENTS

Chiefly Anthea, my wife, for typing the manuscript; Arthur Kemsley (BAA photographs); Bryan Jones (National Air Traffic Services); Roger Cato, Managing Director, Heathrow.

CONTENTS

EXPLANATION OF ABBREVIATIONS

AAIB   Air Accident Investigation Branch

ADM   Airport Duty Manager

ADEM   Airport Duty Engineering Manager

AFS   Airport Fire Service

ASMI   Airfield Surface Movement Indicator

ASU   Airfield Safety Unit

ATC   Air Traffic Control

BAA   British Airports Authority – later BAA plc

BEA   British European Airways

BOAC   British Overseas Airways Corporation

CAA   Civil Aviation Authority

CAT 3   Category 3: meteorological condition of low visibility in fog

DOO   Duty Operations Officer – later Operations Duty Manager

EPIC   Emergency Passenger Information Centre

ERC   Emergency Reception Centre

GMC   Ground Movement Control (ATC)

GSDM   Ground Security Duty Manager

GTDO   Ground Transportation Duty Officer

HAL   Heathrow Airport Ltd. (part of BAA plc)

HOC   Heathrow Operations Centre

IATA   International Air Transport Association

IIB   Incident Information Bureau

ILS   Instrument Landing System

LAS   London Ambulance Service

LATCC London Air Traffic Control Centre

LFB   London Fire Brigade

MT   Motor Transport section

MASU   Manœuvring Area Safety Unit

NATS   National Air Traffic Service

ODM   Operations Duty Manager

PAPI   Precision Approach Path Indicators

PNR   Preferential Noise Routes

RVP   Rendezvous Point

RVR   Runway Visual Range

SADO   Senior Airport Duty Office – later Airport Duty Manager

SDO   Security Duty Officer

TDM   Terminal Duty Manager

TDO   Terminal Duty Officer

VCR   Visual Control Room

VHF   Very High Frequency

VOR   VHF Omni-range – a navigation aid

FOREWORD

by

ROGER CATO
(MANAGING DIRECTOR, HEATHROW AIRPORT)

Well, I know I'd say this, wouldn't I, but I really do believe Heathrow is one of the most interesting and exciting places to work in the UK, and probably in the world.

You can guarantee that with over 60 million people passing through Heathrow airport every year you will see the whole spectrum of travellers, from student backpackers and those in trepidation of their very first flight to the well-heeled businessman in a hurry, pop stars, sporting personalities, Royals and world political leaders.

Over the last 50 years or so, Heathrow has grown from tiny beginnings to the biggest International Airport in the world and it is a major hub for the 'STAR' and 'One World' alliances. Currently, it is staving off the competition from the European hubs, Charles de Gaulle, Frankfurt and Schipol but, in order to stay ahead, it desperately needs permission to build Terminal 5.

On a base of just under 3,000 acres, which is a fraction of the size of most American airports and a sixth of the size of Dallas Fort Worth (which handles roughly the same amount of traffic), the daily operation is frenetic and, to the casual observer, could appear at times to be chaotic. But to those who know airports and specifically Heathrow, like Peter, this is of course seldom the case.

Over the last 10 years there have been significant changes in the airline fleets with the introduction of the latest Airbuses and the Boeing 777, and the new generation of large aircraft poses some significant challenges in terms of creating the infrastructure to handle the large numbers of passengers that they will carry.

The airport is, of course, vital for the UK economy, supporting tens of thousands of jobs, and something like a quarter of the world's major companies have located offices in the Thames Valley because of the close proximity to the huge route network serving Heathrow.

Like so many airports around the world it is not without its problems and, if I had one wish and a magic wand, it would be to reduce the noise generated by arriving traffic, particularly in the early morning.

Peter was one of a number of 'characters' at Heathrow – he was well-known, well-liked and deeply respected for his knowledge of the airline business. I hope you enjoy reading this book, as I have. My only regret is that I always wanted to write a book about the airport and I'm sorry he beat me to it!

INTRODUCTION

Depending on how well you remember your Latin from school you may know that the title I have chosen for this book, "Vivat Heathrow!", means "Long Live Heathrow!" This reflects my personal wish for this great airport, which was very much alive and growing when I left it in 1993; Roger Cato, the Managing Director, assures me this is still so.

The fact that Heathrow exists at all is a cause of grief to a vocal minority which seems to resent aviation in any form and particularly when it generates any noise! This minority acknowledges that Heathrow exists whilst fervently wishing it did not. However I think that most people who have been involved with Heathrow, whether as staff or passengers, admire this Airport, which has very much a personality of its own. It is a world leader in many ways, but particularly in the numbers of international passengers handled. It is a fascinating place to travel through or to work in and is full of **life**. Its main defect, that of being overcrowded at times, arises from there being too little space to cope with the ever-increasing demand from airlines and passengers who like to use Heathrow in preference to other airports. This problem will be largely obviated with the advent of Terminal 5.

Having been based at Heathrow for thirty-five years, the place has inevitably had a significant influence on my life and that of my family. I have been privileged to watch the airport grow, from the North Terminal adjacent to the Bath Road where BOAC and other longhaul carriers operated, to the present, very busy, central terminal area with the more recent addition of Terminal 4 on the south-east side of the airport.

You will gather by now that I am biased in favour of this phenomenon, Heathrow, so I had better explain how I ever became involved with it. Please bear with me whilst I give you a brief account in the first chapter of my 'pre-Heathrow experience' which may go some way to explain my enthusiasm for aviation and Heathrow, or perhaps to confirm the view of the reader that the mind of anyone who enthuses about either is suspect!

I must add a *caveat* here. This book contains only the recollections of a retired aviation man and may unintentionally contain historical and factual inaccuracies due to my fallible memory, for which I apologise in advance to any whom I may thus offend!

CHAPTER ONE

WHY AVIATION?

I was born in 1937 in a remote Indian village in the State of Bihar. My father, a very remarkable doctor, ran a mission hospital which he had virtually designed and built himself. (Rather unusually, my father appears as 'Doctor in Attendance' at my birth on my birth certificate!) My father's work in India was recognised by the British Government which, at the time, ruled India, with the award of two medals. In contrast, but with the same sentiment, an Indian dignitary made a farewell speech in which he thanked Dr Edmunds for "wetting himself in the Indian sun on their behalf." (I think he was referring to perspiration rather than to an embarrassing problem!)

The point in mentioning this early phase in my life is to show that aviation did not feature at all in my formative years. In Hiranpur, my native village, the main forms of transport were bicycles, bullock carts and a few dilapidated lorries and buses. My father did, however, have a Ford A tourer which, by local standards, was very presentable. It was not unknown for vehicles to arrive at the hospital for attention by my father, who was also a competent mechanic and probably had the only decent set of tools in the district. I will mention in passing that, although no aircraft featured in my early days, I did start a lifelong passion for motorcycles because one of my father's partners had a Flat Tank BSA 250 cc which I adored and on which I used to be taken for rides on the rather uncomfortable carrier. To me there has always been an affinity between the thrills of flying and motorcycling; it is probably the sheer sense of freedom.

As was the normal practice for children of British parents working in India, I returned to England in time to start at preparatory school at the age of eight. In those days only the very affluent travelled by air, so we returned by sea from Bombay in a luxury liner the *"SS Andes"* which had been converted into a troop ship. It is probably fortunate that we were forced to go by sea because the vast amounts of baggage we travelled with would never have been accommodated in the aircraft operating in 1946 even if the excess baggage charges could have been met. Apart from the thrill of being on a huge ship, the things on board that most impressed young me were bread, which was white and soft, and butter, which was yellow. The bread I had been used to was coarse and rather dry whilst the butter had been white.

There was nothing spectacular about my days at Prep School and, to my disgust, my school reports, whose arrival at home I dreaded, usually said: 'he could do better if he tried.' I am sure there is some truth in this, but to this very day I have never been able to exert myself in a cause in which I did not believe. At this time learning French and History fell into this category! What I did enthuse about, however, was the building and flying of model aircraft which were powered by small diesel engines. This proved an excellent antidote to academic work, but I was not infrequently in trouble with the powers-that-be because of the awful smells that pervaded the place after my using dope to stretch the aircraft skin, and from the diesel fuel I had to mix myself from castor oil and ether. In spite of all this, I managed to get a minor scholarship to my Public School.

I entered Haileybury and Imperial Service College in 1951 and started life as a 'New Governor'. This title did not convey any elevated status – rather the reverse! You were the lowest form of life and available for 'fagging' duties for any Prefect. The title of Governor dates from the time when Haileybury was the East India College and trained staff for the Indian Civil Service.

Haileybury has since produced many famous aviators, of whom five of the best-known are: The Hon A. Boyle AFC, who holds pilot's certificate No. 13 and was the first British pilot to bank an aircraft off a straight course; Air Chief Marshal Sir Robert Brooke-Popham who flew in the first Squadron to serve overseas in 1914 and was armed only with a revolver; Air Chief Marshal Sir T. Leigh-Mallory of Battle of Britain fame, and two Chiefs of Air Staff, Marshals of the Royal Air Force Slessor and Dixon.

With this magnificent heritage of RAF senior officers behind me I feel I should have excelled in this direction but the highest RAF rank I ever achieved was Corporal in the RAF section of the school's Cadet Corps.

I do, however, owe a great deal to the RAF as, whilst at Haileybury, I learned to fly gliders at RAF Detling in April 1954, where I gained an 'A' & 'B' Gliding Certificate signed by Lord Barbazon of Tara and was later awarded a Flying Scholarship. I was trained on Tiger Moth aircraft at Fair Oaks Aerodrome under the supervision of the Chief Flying Instructor, Wing Commander Cyril Arthur.

The requirements in those days to qualify for a PPL were 15 hours dual and 15 hours solo. The syllabus included spinning and restarting engines in flight, neither of which form part of the current PPL training. In April 1955 the Ministry of Transport and Civil Aviation issued me with a PPL (Flying Machines). The cost of the PPL course was £150 (approximately the cost of one hour's training in 2000). To assist me with my flying training RAF Kenley also supplied a leather helmet, boots and goggles. Arrayed in all this my resemblance to Biggles was stunning!

Fair Oaks Aerodrome was within pedal-cycling distance of my home but, having been left £100 by an elderly aunt (of that generation of aunts, she has been my favourite ever since), I thought a motorcycle to be a more suitable form of transport. I purchased my first motorbike and have hardly been without one since.

Haileybury boys were occasionally let out to explore the countryside on their bicycles (strictly the pedal variety) and the hiring of cars was absolutely forbidden by the school rules. There was no mention of aeroplanes so, when I could afford it, I used to cycle to Panshanger Aerodrome and take friends for flights over the school. The cost was £4 per hour (with no VAT) for a Tiger Moth or Auster! I did not fly too close to the chapel dome as an old Haileyburian Sub-Lieutenant had just been court-marshalled for flying a Westland Wyvern around the chapel at a very low height. I cannot vouch for this, but it was rumoured that the Sub-Lieutenant was given a First Class rail voucher to attend the court marshal whilst the Headmaster was given a Third Class one.

Having somehow gained Science-orientated 'A' Levels I intended, when I left school, to undertake a graduate apprenticeship in Mechanical Engineering with Lister's Diesel Engineers in Dursley, Gloucestershire. At this crucial stage in my life, motorbikes affected my future. When visiting the Lister Apprentice School, I learned that motorbikes were not allowed. Lister's were OUT! Engineering was obviously not for me but my fascination with aircraft remained.

Whilst watching aircraft at RAF North Weald, a friend and I must have penetrated rather too far through the perimeter fence and were picked up by a patrol vehicle and taken to the Guard Room. Our excuse (rapidly thought up) was that we were there to enquire about flying careers. In my case at least, there was an element of truth in this excuse as I later applied for a Short Service Commission in the Fleet Air Arm. I was, in any case, liable for National Service so I volunteered for the Royal Navy. The alternative of being conscripted into the Army was too awful to contemplate. I had a short taste of the Army in the school's Cadet Corps. I mean no disrespect to the Army but I do not think we would have got on!

After what seemed an age, Their Lordships of the Admiralty invited me and some thirty other aspiring aviators to a three-day selection course at RNAS Lee-on-Solent. As far as I can remember, only three of us survived and were taken to Portsmouth to have our hearing assessed.

I clearly remember the Chief Petty Officer, who was carrying out the test, saying to me: "Do you play a musical instrument, Sir?"

When I replied in the negative, he said: "I should not bother, Sir, you are high tone deaf."

This destroyed any aspirations I may have had of earning my living as a concert pianist or, in fact, of being used on anti-submarine duties where the ability to distinguish between sounds close to one another in frequency is essential. But I was so thrilled to be accepted for flying that I could live with my lack of musical talent.

I joined The Royal Navy on a cold day in January 1956. My fellow Aviation Cadets and I reported to Portland Harbour resplendent in our officer uniforms. Any pride we may have had at that time was rapidly destroyed by an encounter with our Petty Officer. The gist of his welcome to the Senior Service was that "he had been lumbered with us and that we would learn to hate his guts."

This Petty Officer was a Gunnery Instructor which, for those not familiar with The Royal Navy, is something akin to the Sergeant Major in the Army – he thrives on parade grounds and delights in screaming abuse at anyone under his orders, but particularly Officer Cadets.

Having received our welcome from this fierce man, we were then faced with the problem of boarding our ship, the aircraft carrier HMS Theseus. HMS Theseus was a Light Fleet Carrier of 23,000 tons and formed part of the Royal Navy Home Fleet Training Squadron, and was commanded by Captain E. Pizey RN.

We had assembled at the bottom of the gangway with our luggage, which included a large metal cabin trunk. Somehow we were expected to get all this and ourselves up to the top of the gangway, salute the ship and then descend almost vertical ladders to our accommodation in the bowels of the ship. The dilemma was whether to lower the trunk down the ladder in front of you or to drag it behind you. Both options seemed perilous but it is amazing what fear can achieve! We were more afraid of the Petty Officer barking at us than of breaking our necks.

Thankfully, we all arrived intact in our new home which we were to spend a great deal of the next six months cleaning. Having settled in and found somewhere to sling our hammocks, we then had to dress for dinner. This brought with it a new problem – Her Majesty had graciously provided each of us with 'wing' collars and double-ended bow ties to be worn at dinner in the Gunroom – as the junior officers' mess was known. None of us was competent in dealing with such ties, and anyone who has experienced similar problems will know how useless it is to look in the mirror.

As with all future problems, we Cadets helped each other through. Such co-operation was usually designed to thwart our tormentor, the omnipresent Petty Officer.

The six months on board HMS Theseus were, in retrospect, great fun and even our Petty Officer revealed himself to have a kind centre and not to be the ogre he liked us to consider him. He did a good job in turning what he described as a "miserable shower" (one of his less profane descriptions) into tolerably smart junior officers.

Our training at sea was attuned to our future in aviation so, when we were not doing drill, funeral drill, cleaning the ship or learning to be sailors, we were taught such subjects as aerodynamics, meteorology and aircraft navigation.

At the end of the six months we sat several examinations and tests on such things as reading Morse code and semaphore. As a class we were all hopeless at semaphore, the reading of waving flags and I confess that we all cheated. Our instructor obviously despaired of us and whispered the answers to us. I never, after that, had any cause to read semaphore.

The majority of us survived and became officers, much to the expressed surprise of our Petty Officer who continued to the last to teach us funeral drill. This showed his great lack of faith in naval aviation in general, and us in particular!

After a further short period at sea we should have gone on to flying training but this was interrupted by the Suez War. I was on Euston station hoping to go on holiday when I was summoned by the Tannoy to report to the Stationmaster's office. Wondering who in the family had died, I rushed there, to be told to report within twelve hours to HMS Ocean which was sailing almost immediately. I really had not anticipated this – I was going to war!

I rushed home, packed, took a train to Portsmouth and reported, as ordered, to HMS Ocean, a sister ship to HMS Theseus which I had just left. The ship sailed almost immediately for Malta carrying a large contingent of the Army with all their vehicles and equipment. The aircraft carrier's flight deck was covered in military vehicles. In Malta we embarked Royal Marine Commandos and sailed for Limassol, Cyprus, where most of the Army disembarked. We then went on to Famagusta to disembark the remaining troops. I was sent ashore to patrol the dockyard with a large revolver, a Land Rover and four sailors in case we encountered any terrorist activity. I am for ever grateful that I did not come across a terrorist as I think I would have been at more risk of injury from my revolver than any enemy!

The ship then sailed to Suez and we all braced ourselves for war – imagine a tin hat and battledress we were required to wear, in the Mediterranean! There was a great sense of occasion followed by a complete anticlimax when someone in a high place cancelled the war without consulting us! We learned later that America had brought pressure to bear on the British to back off.

Having escaped risking our lives in battle with the Egyptians, we returned in a leisurely manner to the UK where, having disembarked, I effectively lost contact with the 'watery' side of the Royal Navy, although in naval uniform I was to spend the rest of my service on RAF stations.

I was first posted to RAF Syerston, near Newark, Nottinghamshire where I was trained on the Percival Provost T.1. This was a delightful monoplane with 'taildragger' undercarriage and was powered by a supercharged 550 hp Alvis Leonides radial engine. At Syerston we got used to the RAF's rather more relaxed approach to parades and ceremonials. However, to ensure we did not slacken off there was a Senior Naval Officer on the station. The Provost course included aerobatics, formation flying and low flying, which I had not experienced in the PPL course.

After successfully completing the course at Syerston (120 hours flying), we were sent to RAF Valley in Anglesea for jet training. Early training was undertaken in two-seat de Havilland Vampire T.11s, and later we progressed to the single-seat Vampire FB.5 and FB.9 which, unlike the T.11, had no ejector seats. I loved flying the Vampire and, in addition to being given flying pay, I seemed to be given an abundant supply of Penguin biscuits and coffee.

Life seemed too good to be true, when disaster struck. It was found, during an instrument flying check, that I was momentarily unconscious. I was sent for testing to the Royal Naval Air Medical Establishment, Seafield Park, near Lee-on-Solent, and thence to the RAF Medical Establishment at Farnborough, where I did some flying in Meteor 8s with pilots who were also doctors. Tests found some incompatibility between myself and low pressure oxygen. I was finished on jets and my Civilian Pilot's Licence was endorsed and limited to aircraft for which I did not need to wear an oxygen mask. My flying career in The Royal Navy was over abruptly, leaving me in some disarray as to what I should do next.

Whilst contemplating the future, I consoled myself by trading in an aged AJS motorcycle for a new Triumph Speed Twin – a magnificent maroon 500 cc, such as then used by the police.

CHAPTER TWO

BRITISH OVERSEAS AIRWAYS CORPORATION

When one has been prevented from earning a living by flying aircraft, any alternative occupation seems very mundane. I considered all sorts of possibilities, including offering myself to the Church of England which, I am thankful, did not accept me. My other great enthusiasm after flying – motorcycles – did not offer any obvious career for me so I investigated what the air transport industry had to offer.

My only experience at this time of civil air transport was a pleasure flight in a de Havilland Rapide, G-AEWL, operated by Trans Channel Airways at Ramsgate. I was on holiday there at the age of 14 and saw advertised pleasure flights for 15 shillings. The Edmunds family of four took to the air for the first time! All I really remember of that flight was the extremely bumpy take-off from what seemed just a farmer's field, and the fact that a large North Country lady bumped her head on entering the minibus taking us to the airfield. What impressed me was not the discomfort of the lady in question but the lack of sympathy of her companion, who observed: "Never mind, where there's no sense there's no feeling!" This probably also accounted for the fact that I have never since been afraid of flying.

With this vast experience of civil air transport behind me I wrote to BOAC offering them my services and waited . . . and waited. I knew a senior BOAC Captain who enquired how I was getting on with my application and when he heard that little appeared to be happening, he promised to visit the Personnel Department – with almost immediate results. As I was to discover later, senior BOAC Captains were, in those days, afforded almost God-like status by all other airline employees.

I was invited by BOAC to attend a three-day selection board for training as a Station Officer. It sounded rather like a railway job but, having found out what a Station Officer was, I attended. Station Officers were staff, normally overseas, who were in charge of BOAC's operations at an airport. The most senior was the Station Manager. Next came the Senior Station Officer and then Station Duty Officers who usually worked on a shift basis. In my time in BOAC these staff were almost invariably British.

The Station Office Trainee Scheme had been started by Imperial Airways and was continued by its successor, BOAC. The idea was to select young well-educated men to be given a thorough training in all aspects of the airline to equip them to represent BOAC in all parts of the world. It also provided a pool of expertise from which future senior management could be selected.

The selection board was held at Dormy House, a delightful country house adjacent to a golf course in Sunningdale. The selection process was very similar to the officer selection I had undergone in the Royal Navy. In those days the men who represented BOAC abroad were also in a sense ambassadors for the UK. Most of those selected for interview were graduates or had recently held commissions in one of the armed services. BOAC had to ensure that those they sent abroad were not only very competent at their job but did not let the side down socially. To this end, we always ate with our selectors to ensure we did not eat our peas off our knives!

I was accepted for training by BOAC but there was an interval of some months during which I had to find something to do to provide myself with an income. I did two jobs during this period – one was as a baker's roundsman which caused great embarrassment to some of my lady neighbours who used to come to the door with their hair in curlers not expecting to meet someone they knew socially. It was also very interesting to see how different people treated tradesmen.

The second job was as a tractor driver on a market garden. Essentially the task was to collect and transport crates of vegetables which had been packed in the fields by a team of women who arrived daily from the East End of London. I learned a lot of words from them that I had not heard, even in the Navy! On this job I met an ex-RAF pilot and, through sheer boredom, the two of us used to experiment with our tractors until we accidentally damaged some crates of radishes. We were both sacked, and since then I always omitted this fact from any job application!

My fortunes then changed as, through the kindness of Fred Newman, Chairman of DAN-AIR, I was allowed to operate as a supernumerary crew member on Avro York aircraft, G-ANTI and G-ANTK (the latter is now under restoration at Duxford), which were chartered to carry RAF spares between UK and Singapore. This also enabled me to stop off in Calcutta to visit my parents.

The Avro York was a freighter derivative of the Lancaster bomber and, like the Lancaster, had four Rolls-Royce Merlin engines. The aircraft was unpressurised and cruised at just over 200 kt, which meant that the journey from the UK (RAF Lyneham) to Singapore took a considerable time. The same crew operated throughout, so flying mostly took place during the daytime with overnight stops in hotels *en route*. These night stops were usually Rome, Habbaniyah (near Baghdad), Karachi and Calcutta. The performance of a laden York was not impressive and, unless you were airborne very early in the morning in places like Karachi, the temperature would prevent your take-off. If you did get airborne, you then had to cross the desert at 10,000 ft in a very noisy aircraft which was being buffeted by the hot air currents rising off the baking earth beneath.

In-flight catering in the York was interesting. If hot food was required, this was achieved by suspending tins on a string and lowering them into a water boiler attached to the bulkhead behind the flightdeck. When the tins were hot you opened them with great caution because of the low pressure inside the aircraft. One of the Captains would only drink English milk and would start the journey from UK with a large container of it and was not deterred by the fact that it rapidly became revolting! The York did not have the luxury of a refrigerator.

I shall always be grateful to DAN-AIR for giving me the experience of charter flying. The enthusiasm of the crews was tremendous and Captains did not consider such functions as removing wheel chocks to be beneath their dignity.

At last, in October 1958, I arrived at Heathrow and, with fifteen others, I reported to the BOAC headquarters building (normally referred to as the 'Kremlin') in Heathrow's No. 1 Maintenance area. The 'Kremlin' consisted of four enormous aircraft hangars with office accommodation super-imposed above. The building is still in use but has been much extended to accommodate the B.747s and looks very different from the original.

The three-year course we, as Station Officer Trainees, were embarked upon must be the best provided by any airline in the world. Station Officer Trainees belonged to the Traffic Department reporting to Denis Bustard,

Traffic Manager. We were required to wear uniforms similar to those worn by Cadets in The Royal Navy. After satisfactorily passing exams and completing 1½ years as Station Officer Trainees, we were promoted to Provisional Station Officer and wore lapel patches on our uniforms, like Royal Navy Midshipmen. On finishing the three-year course, we were given three gold strips on our sleeve. On completion of the course some elected to concentrate on selling BOAC abroad as District Sales Officers.

The course covered all aspects of the airline's operations and we had to pass examinations at an advanced level in Ticket Issue and Fare Construction, Reservations, Aircraft Loading and Loadsheet preparation, Flight Planning & Radio Communications and Navigation. Added to that we covered all the syllabus of the Commercial Pilot's Licence.

We were trained in one task which we were never likely to perform. We did a week of cabin service training which involved serving meals in an aircraft – fortunately this was in a mock-up fuselage and the meals were not served to genuine passengers.

Apart from being required to pass all the above, BOAC stressed, above all, the vital importance of good service to our customers, whether they be passengers, cargo shippers, agents or Royal Mail (always afforded the highest priority).

From the first day with BOAC we were continually told that this was the best airline in the world, and I still believe this to be true. To enjoy working for an organisation one has to be proud of it and this was certainly true of all BOAC staff. The service given to passengers was superb, both in the air and on the ground (there was less emphasis on profits then). As Trainees we did a lot of flying world-wide and experienced this service for ourselves.

When space was available we usually managed to get up-graded to First Class.

In addition to our airline-related training, we were required to obtain a Diploma in Business Administration; this was done at Ealing Technical College. The best part of the 'Trainee' course was gaining practical experience in actually doing the job. Some of this took place at Heathrow but the majority was at foreign airports. Much as I like Heathrow, overseas postings were more interesting and financially rewarding. We were accommodated in First Class hotels and given an overseas allowance as well!

For my first overseas posting I was sent back to my native land to work at Dum-Dum Airport, Calcutta. I was housed in the Great Eastern Hotel, a real relic of the British Raj! I sometimes wonder about the idleness of some of our forefathers in India – the hotel servants were so attentive that your trousers were held out for you to step into! In reality it is much easier to do it on your own, and this I did.

Calcutta in 1958 was still very British and I found to my embarrassment that I was invited to join a Club which my BOAC Area Manager was unable to get admitted to. The reason was my Haileybury College Old Boys tie! This would not, I think, have enhanced my career prospects.

Calcutta Airport, Dum-Dum, was a real culture shock after Heathrow. The buildings were rather 'tired' and the electricity supply most unreliable. Landside areas of the terminal were full of men squatting around in the hope of portering duties or of being able to sell some aspect of the 'mystic East' to a gullible American tourist. Some of these men had pronounced squints and this led to one of my early experiences of the great resourcefulness of my Indian colleagues.

Some tourists used to try to 'do' India in a few days and were overcome by the culture shock. One night a couple refused to board the BOAC Britannia to London although they had progressed as far as the departure lounge. The lady complained that an "evil eye" had been put on her husband and she insisted on it being removed by a doctor. It was by this time nearly midnight and the Captain was fretting because of the possible delay to the aircraft departure. There was no possibility of finding a doctor so one of the staff borrowed a white coat from the restaurant and apparently played the part of the doctor sufficiently well for the couple to board the flight. All that had happened to cause this problem was an encounter with an unfortunate airport resident with a very bad squint.

I am not naturally given to deceit but, as in the case above, India at times drove you to it. By Indian Government regulations all food unloaded from our aircraft, because it had not been consumed in flight, had to be destroyed. At the front of the airport were refuse bins in which children and dogs were scavenging for food. Instead of being destroyed, some superb BOAC dinners found their way to these children.

The route from landside to airside was via a fairly narrow corridor where a large Indian Customs lady sat at a desk in front of which you had to pass. She used to sit there chewing betel nut, the remains of which she would expertly spit onto the wall opposite. As a result, you learned to time your transit past her desk with some care, especially if you heard her clearing her throat!

One of the greatest problems of operating through Eastern airports in those days was the poor communications. Calcutta lies approximately half-way along the routes joining London & Sydney and London & Hong Kong. If the flight was delayed at a previous station, the message to that effect often did not reach Calcutta before the scheduled arrival time of the aircraft, nor at times did the Load Message. This is a statement from the previous airport as to what load is on the aircraft for each destination, and from this you deduce how much load and how many passengers you can put on the aircraft at your airport. Thus, in the absence of this vital information, all passengers booked were checked in on the assumption that the flight was on schedule and that they could all be accommodated. Difficult problems arose when such assumptions proved false and passengers were seriously delayed or off-loaded.

In spite of my comments above on communications problems I must emphasize that BOAC did look after delayed passengers extremely well and placed Airport passenger staff in the hotel to help them. Also, to improve on the available communications links BOAC installed its own network worldwide (the Overseas Fixed Telecommunications System). Even this system had difficulties unforeseen by BOAC. The landline link between Delhi and Calcutta failed and I was told that investigations revealed that the copper wire was being used by some village entrepreneur to make ornaments!

Calcutta, as a city, had few redeeming features as I remember it. It was hot, dirty and overcrowded, with many of the citizens living in abject poverty. This resulted in one being accosted by beggars every time one stepped out of the hotel. For me, this very much reduced the pleasure of living in a luxury hotel. That said, I do remember Calcutta for the delightful Indian staff at the airport and for the fact that you could order a glass of beer at a bar. This you could not do in Bombay or New Delhi, where I worked later. In Bombay if you wanted a beer you had first to be registered as an 'alcoholic,' and in New Delhi you had to obtain a beer by having it delivered to your hotel room in a *dhobi* (laundry) basket. The hotels all had lavish bars which could not be used!

In early 1959 I was posted to Bahrain airport, on loan to Air Services Gulf, and was accommodated in Speedbird House. Because of the lack of good hotels in many places to which they operated, BOAC set up their own Speedbird Houses, mainly to accommodate their flight crews, although they were also available to the public.

Bahrain consists of two islands, with the town on one and the airport on the other. The two are joined by a causeway which is closed to traffic at night to enable shipping to pass. This had the unfortunate result that if you were delayed at the airport because of a late aircraft you were there for the night. At the time, there was still an RAF squadron of Scottish Aviation Twin Pioneer aircraft based at the airport. The RAF had an outdoor Astra cinema which was of great benefit if you were stuck at the airport overnight.

In Bahrain, we looked after many airlines, apart from BOAC, but particularly QANTAS and the many British charter airlines then operating, such as Derby Airways, Skyways, Hunting Clan, DAN-AIR, British Commonwealth Air Services, etc. Many of these airlines were using fairly aged aircraft such as Yorks, Tudors, DC-3s and DC-4s, and early versions of the Constellation 749s (which had previously belonged to BOAC). Some of the aircraft had been employed on the Berlin Airlift and used to have not infrequent delays for mechanical reasons. The national airline, Gulf Aviation (now Gulf Air), then operated a fleet of de Havilland Herons and Doves and flew only within the Gulf area in contrast to the large international fleet it now has. Gulf Aviation was founded in 1950 by an Englishman called Freddy Bosworth who flew out to Bahrain with a war surplus Avro Anson and load of ex-RAF spares.

Like many Gulf states, Bahrain seemed to have a disproportionate number of citizens who were part of the ruling or Royal family. In one such state, which I will not name, an elderly and rather eccentric member of the ruling family used to arrive at the airport without a ticket and board the aircraft for London. Because of his status none of the immigration or police authorities would take any action. We therefore allowed all passengers to board and the Captain would then apologise that the aircraft was indefinitely delayed for technical reasons. The dignitary would then be escorted back to his Rolls-Royce and, after a decent interval, the aircraft departed.

Bahrain was also my first introduction to Haj flights – flights taking pilgrims to Mecca. Special charter flights are arranged at a particular time of the year to carry these pilgrims. Most of them had never travelled by air and arrived at the airport with equipment more suitable for setting up camp. The state of the aircraft interior after these flight defies description. It was not their fault, but most of these passengers were not familiar with western sanitary arrangements.

After a few enjoyable months in Bahrain, I went to somewhere totally different – Tokyo. The first thing that struck me about Tokyo was the fact that many restaurants, bars etc. were labelled 'On' or 'Off' Limits; this, I soon discovered, applied to American military personnel who were still much in evidence. I was also struck by the contrast between the very aggressive and apparently suicidal way in which the Japanese drove their cars and their very gracious and courteous behaviour when you met them face to face.

My posting to Tokyo was mainly to learn the marketing side of the airline but I also spent some time with the engineers at Haneda, the Tokyo airport then in use. BOAC, at this time, was the only airline operating through Tokyo whose aircraft did not use petrol, the jet engine having arrived in the Britannias and Comets. As a result, in all Tokyo bars would be found tins of cigarette lighter fuel labelled thus: "Please help yourself to this petrol – free. BOAC DOES NOT USE IT ANY MORE."

Part of our training in Tokyo, as mentioned before, was to be attached to the engineering department and, to this end, we spent time with the Station Engineer who explained his side of the BOAC station operation. The inbound BOAC flights from Hong Kong used to arrive at approximately midday and, after the passengers and deadload had been removed, the aircraft was towed to the engineering base where it remained overnight. Invariably there was plenty of food still on board so, on a fine day, we would sit on the wing enjoying a picnic lunch and finishing off unconsumed champagne. I hasten to add, we also did some work as well.

Japan I found to be a fascinating place, both in its beauty and very different culture. Japanese passengers are probably the easiest of any to deal with as they are very well disciplined and polite. They are so polite that sometimes it is difficult to hurry them onto an aircraft when they are bidding farewell to friends, as they bow up and down interminably. How nice a problem this is to deal with compared with the western problem of loutish behaviour and 'air rage.'

Tokyo was also a shopper's paradise. The department stores were magnificent and contained all the electronic gadgets which were just emerging in that country and had not yet reached the West. I bought myself the first tiny Sony transistor radio I had ever seen. I cannot fault the radio but it caused me great problems with Indian Customs when I later stopped off in New Delhi. For some reason they wanted to impound it!

To enable us to understand the country better, another Trainee and I were sent to a village near Miki-moto, where cultured pearls are produced. On arrival at our inn, we were met at the door by our host and each presented with a dressing gown, a pair of slippers and a toothbrush, reminiscent of the thing I used to polish brass with in the Navy. The dressing gown I could just manage, the slippers were about half the size needed for my big feet and, fortunately, I had my own toothbrush.

The bedroom was almost entirely bare and one slept on matting on the floor. Meals were served very graciously in the bedroom but the content was not really to my taste. There was great emphasis on raw fish or squid. For breakfast we were given tepid fish soup, into which a raw egg had been dropped!

The next culture shock was the communal bath. This was a small pool heated from underneath, in which the residents sat cooking together after having first washed themselves with soap and a bucket of water. A cubicle was provided for washing but you then emerged naked by the side of the pool full of impassive Japanese faces – the rest of their bodies being totally submerged. You had the choice of providing a spectacle to the mixed group in the bath or of being scalded on jumping in! It was a very interesting outing and we returned to Tokyo very clean and extremely hungry.

I then spent a period at Heathrow working as a Passenger Officer. Life was much more genteel in those days, with no queuing or security checks. The tedious business of checking was sometimes undertaken by the chauffeur and it was even known for passengers to request a seat at the Captain's table. As a Passenger Officer, much of my time was spent looking after VIPs in the Monarch Lounge, which enabled me to meet many famous people. BOAC's prestige flight to New York was the 'Monarch' operated daily by a Stratocruiser.

It was also at this time that BOAC transferred its operations from the Northside Terminal to the newly-constructed Oceanic Terminal, in the central area of Heathrow. The Oceanic Terminal, Arrivals and Departures, was entirely contained within what is now the Departures Building of Terminal 3. Even in the new terminal, life was relatively relaxed with everyone's efforts directed to obtaining an 'on schedule' departure. Passenger loads were very small by today's standards and, if flights were delayed, passengers could be given individual attention, including free telegrams to advise those meeting them of the delay. If delays were prolonged, passengers might be taken to the theatre in London and, if sent to an hotel, a member of BOAC's staff stayed in the hotel with them to assist them.

I was in England long enough to meet and get engaged to the lovely girl I later married before I was sent on my travels again. This time it was to Bombay – I seem to have a homing instinct for India. My spell in Bombay was during the monsoon when it was not only infernally hot and humid but I was expected to visit all our travel agents and encourage them to sell BOAC in preference to other airlines. This inevitably involved me in drinking huge quantities of tea. It was not tea as we are used to in England. This tea had been brewing for some time in the kettle with the milk and sugar already mixed in. Every agent I called upon would provide tea and it would have been very ungracious to refuse. What I suffered to gain business for BOAC!

Bombay was a much nicer city to live in than Calcutta; although poverty was still in evidence it was less overt. My stay in Bombay ended with a serious talk with the Area Manager who advised me against getting married for I was far too young. I am glad I ignored this!

From Bombay I was posted to Jan Smutts airport, Johannesburg. This was a very pleasant change from extreme heat to a delightful climate, beautiful countryside and good food. The airport was also fairly modern but even there I was very conscious that I was treated differently because I was white. My first *faux pas* was to walk into a toilet for black ladies. There were adjacent doors, one labelled 'Ladies,' and in my haste I assumed that the next one must be 'Gents.' If nothing else I emerged wiser and provided some merriment for the ladies within.

The flights between Heathrow and Johannesburg were, at the time, operated by Comet 4 aircraft. There were several stops *en route* at such places as Rome, Cairo, Khartoum, Nairobi and Salisbury (now Harare). The BOAC Manager at the airport had previously been a flying boat captain and had somehow acquired a radio set from one of these aircraft and installed it in the office. Thus we were able to monitor the aircraft's progress without being dependent on the official communications system which had the same deficiencies as that in India.

One significant event occurred whilst I was at Jan Smutts. There was a great reception at the airport for the return of Dr Verwoerd after he had withdrawn South Africa from the British Commonwealth. It is the only occasion I have seen field guns on an airport apron giving a 21-gun salute.

The BEA Vanguard was, at this time, doing its tropical trials at Johannesburg and one day brought Jan Smutts to a halt by doing a heavy landing and bursting all main wheel tyres in the middle of the runway.

At the airport we had a delightful Traffic Assistant, a Zulu called Samuel. His job was in reality to be a very efficient clerk, ensuring that everything was ready for handling a flight. He was invaluable in being the only person who knew where to find things! He lived with his family in a settlement outside the city and had to come to work in a 'Blacks Only' train. I am afraid some of BOAC's milk from the aircraft found its way through us to Samuel's children. Much out of character, Samuel was late for work one day and I later found a letter on my desk: "Dear Sir, I am very sorry I was late this morning but the train went without me," signed "Samuel, General Adviser to BOAC."

One of Samuel's tasks was to take on board the aircraft documents (ship's papers) and these were always only ready at the very last minute. On one occasion Samuel was still on board delivering the papers when the steps were withdrawn from the aircraft by the staff of South African Airways, who did ramp handling on behalf of BOAC. Samuel appeared at the aircraft door but the ramp staff refused to reposition the steps for a 'black'. The problem was resolved but the incident does show the then prevailing attitude to black people.

Samuel had been such a help to me that, when I left I offered to buy him something. He was a local preacher in the settlement in which he lived and asked for a new prayer book as his current one was falling apart. I was delighted to supply him with a new one and, on receiving it, he was so thrilled that he saluted me simultaneously with both hands!

I then returned to England and, after a short posting to Manchester Ringway Airport, I married Anthea Samuelson, to whom I am still happily attached, on the 24th September 1960. Our first posting abroad as a couple was to Basle/Mulhouse airport to cover the winter period. BOAC flights did not operate into Basle but it is an indication of how highly BOAC rated passenger service. A BOAC representative had to be available in Basle in case fog at Zurich airport should cause a BOAC flight to divert into Basle. In the four months we were in Basle, I was only needed on thirteen occasions.

When Zurich was fogbound, flights of many airlines apart from BOAC descended on Basle airport and the small team of Swissair staff could only cope with the bare essentials such as loading and offloading baggage. My being there was to provide the individual attention to the passengers whose journey plans had been disrupted, and to sort out the crew. Not infrequently, diversions and consequent delays resulted in crewing problems. On longhaul routes there is an intricate system of crew planning where a fresh crew takes an aircraft over from the incoming crew at an *en route* airport. Any disruption to the schedule at one point can have repercussions all down the route because the operating hours of crews are strictly regulated.

Switzerland was a beautiful place in which to spend a winter but, apart from the thirteen occasions mentioned, I had very little work to do except from daily consultation over the telephone with the Zurich Met. Office – the phone number is still engraved in my memory.

After Switzerland I was sent back to India again, but this time with a wife. My wife had never been to India before and was in difficulties almost as soon as she arrived in New Delhi. She arrived in a Comet 4 in the early hours of the morning when, even then, the heat is oppressive after England. Her new home was a company flat with resident cook (bearer) who had his quarters near the kitchen at the back of the building. The custom was for the lady of the house (the *memsahib*) to brief the cook each day as to what food he should buy in the market and to give him the money. He was also responsible for maintaining a supply of water that had been boiled, for drinking. The cook was duly briefed and I went off to work at Palam airport leaving my wife time to settle in. During the afternoon I received a telephone call from a rather concerned wife who said there was no drinking water nor was there any sign of the cook, nor of lunch. Investigations revealed that the cook had indeed been shopping but, instead of buying food, had supplied himself with a quantity of locally-produced alcohol! In any event, he was fast asleep at the back of the house. The wife of another BOAC staff member with rather more experience of India came to assist and the cook was dismissed. Without any further ado on our part, the former cook's brother arrived and assumed the cook's responsibilities as though nothing had happened.

Thereafter, the household ran satisfactorily and we even entertained on occasions. Because we were only on a short posting we obviously did not have with us any superior tableware, silver candlesticks etc. When we gave our first dinner we were surprised to find that several such items appeared. These had apparently been borrowed by the cook from fellow bearers in neighbouring houses to ensure the Edmunds did not let standards drop!

When security was mentioned in this era it had little to do with terrorism or searching passengers but with theft from aircraft holds. The BOAC aircraft passing through Delhi were usually on the ground for some 45 minutes but, during this period, some very skillful thefts occurred. High-value consignments of such things as watches were shipped in wooden boxes sealed with steel bands. During the transit through Delhi the label would be removed, a small hole cut through the wood sufficient to withdraw the watches, after which the label was replaced over the hole and the package continued to its destination empty but apparently intact. Crates of whisky in transit in airport 'bonded stores' suffered a similar fate. A small hole was drilled in the bottom of the bottle and the contents removed.

The bottle was then refilled with cold tea and the base sealed. It was not until some unfortunate poured himself a tot that the substitution came to light – probably many miles from Delhi.

The BOAC staff at Delhi airport were delightful and had a great sense of humour. They were very loyal to the British which, on occasions, I found difficult. Many of the Ramp staff were retired Ghurka soldiers who were used to serving under British Army officers and, because I was dressed in a military-style uniform, they would leap to their feet and salute every time I passed. When there were no aircraft around they would squat in the shade outside my office door. Thus, every time I came in or out, I had to be subjected to this performance.

At the time I was in Delhi there was a lot of gold smuggling; Indian Customs were particularly thorough and all flights and cabin staff were subjected to special scrutiny. Flights could not be cleared to depart from Delhi without Customs permission and they could refuse permission without giving a reason. When we protested we were told that we, the British, wrote the regulations to which they adhered. You couldn't win.

The BOAC crews used to stop in the Ashoka hotel for a break before continuing down the route. One of the stewardesses, whilst in the hotel, received a call from one of the airport Customs officers who wished to take her out. He had obviously seen her on arrival at the airport and obtained her name from the 'General Declaration' – a list of operating crew required by Customs. She declined his offer and, when the flight on which she was to leave Delhi was due to depart, the same man refused clearance. He was not required to say why, but it was obvious to us. My usual ploy on these occasions was to involve or threaten to involve the British Air Attaché from the Embassy; it worked!

One example of the calibre of the Indian staff was a Mr Singh Rai. He was on duty one busy night shift and responsible for doing the Flight Plans for several flights. This task required quick and accurate mathematical work. This particular night he didn't seem his usual cheerful self so I enquired what was wrong. He told me that he had an insect right down inside his ear which was scratching around and obviously unable to reverse out. I suggested he go and seek immediate medical assistance but he said it had happened before and he would get it removed in the morning when his shift finished.

At the end of my three-year course I was a fully-qualified Station Officer and sported three gold rings on my uniform sleeve in place of the 'Midshipman' patches I wore as a Probationary Station Officer. Thus attired, I was posted to Dorval Airport, Montreal. The job there was almost exclusively concerned with Flight Planning, Flight Watch and Pressure Pattern Analysis.

Amongst many interesting aircraft types based at Dorval at this time were several PBY Catalina aircraft which had been suitably adapted for fighting bush fires.

BOAC was then operating Britannia 312 and DC-7C aircraft between the UK and Montreal. The DC-7C aircraft were in freighter configuration, sometimes entirely filled with cages of monkeys gathered from Asia and brought to Canada for medical research. It was a traffic I very much disliked being involved with on two counts; firstly I was desperately sorry for the little creatures and secondly the smell on board the aircraft was dreadful.

The Britannias were very sensitive to weather conditions and particularly to temperature. In unfavourable conditions the westbound aircraft did not have sufficient fuel to reach Montreal and diverted to Halifax, Monkton or Gander. For eastbound flights Montreal would prepare flight plans at various pressure levels and tracks to obtain the most fuel-efficient; this was quite a long process with no computer assistance as is available now. Having established the fuel required for the Montreal-London sector we then added extra fuel for possible diversion or holding. If weather conditions were unsatisfactory Captains elected to take extra fuel above that already loaded. This in turn often resulted in passengers with firm bookings and cargo being off-loaded. The task of telling the unfortunate passengers so affected often fell to me!

I mentioned earlier the overly deferential way in which BOAC Captains were treated. They stayed, for example, in different hotels from the rest of the crew when at foreign cities. Most of these Captains were very pleasant and did not let this treatment go to their heads but inevitably there were some who were insufferably arrogant. One such Captain, whilst in an hotel, called the local BOAC Manager at home to complain that the early morning cup of tea served to him was not hot! This sort of attitude did not go down well with Canadian staff and when one particularly difficult Captain was operating a flight from Dorval, two ground engineers saw him drop a sweet paper on the floor of the flight deck. He then called the Station Engineer to complain that his aircraft had not been cleaned properly. This time there were two witnesses against him. His Flight Manager dealt with the matter.

In 1978, when I later did a Flying Instructor course at Blackbushe, I had, as my instructor, one of the BOAC Britannia 312 Captains who, having retired from the airline, had been appointed to the panel of Instructor Examiners for the UK. He was, externally, rather a stern man with half-moon glasses, who smoked small cigars. His method of teaching you to be an instructor was, or so it appeared to me, to so demoralise you initially by persuading you of your inability to fly that you felt like giving up. He then built you up again to the standard he required. He boasted that he had had no failures. If someone was not likely to pass, he stopped the training quickly. Fortunately, he and I got on very well and I passed my Instructor test at Biggin Hill, examined by a British Caledonian Captain. Understanding airline Captains probably helped!

My next posting was back to Johannesburg again and, whilst there, I saw a vacancy notice for a Traffic Inspector in British European Airways. (BOAC and BEA always advertised each others' vacancies and shared the same pension scheme, so transfer between the two was fairly simple.) This post was two grades senior to me, but I applied and returned to London, First Class, on the Comet for the interview at BEA Headquarters in Bealine House, Ruislip.

To my surprise, I was offered the job and left Longhaul operations in BOAC for Shorthaul in BEA in 1962.

CHAPTER THREE

BRITISH EUROPEAN AIRWAYS

When I joined British European Airways as a Traffic Inspector in 1962, I was one of five and, between us, we divided up all the countries to which BEA operated and were then responsible for visiting all the airports within those areas and reporting on, not only the airline's staff performance, but the airport facilities provided by the controlling Airport Authority.

The entire summer was spent carrying out these inspections and other special projects allocated to us (mine was the introduction of the Trident – of which more later). The countries for which I was responsible were Norway, Sweden, Finland, Austria, Germany, Malta, Libya, Czechoslovakia, Greece, Israel, Poland, USSR and – to help keep things in perspective – Scotland!

Depending on the size of the airport being visited, these inspections normally involved being away two or three nights and this gave one a good opportunity to see the local area. The BEA Station Superintendents were always most hospitable (at this stage they had not seen the report!), and usually showed us all the items of special local interest. In those days, there was often a town terminal where passengers could check in for their flights, and these were also subject to our inspection.

As you might imagine, the efficiency of airport operations varied from place to place. In general, Scandinavia, Germany, Austria and Israel were good. By their omission, you may gather that others did sometimes fall short of perfection. Scotland was a case on its own, on which I shall enlarge later.

During the winter, the Traffic Inspectors had two functions. The most time-consuming one was acting as instructors at the Traffic Training Unit at Heston. Here we were required to be expert in all aspects of traffic handling, e.g. Passenger Service, Ticketing, Fare Construction, Cargo Documentation & Customs Clearance, Aircraft Loading and completion of Load Sheets and Balance Charts. These skills we had to impart to staff from all over the BEA network, some of whom did not have a very good grasp of the English language. I am now quite convinced that the finest way of learning any subject is to have to teach it.

Our second winter duty was to set and carry out promotion exams for Traffic staff throughout the UK, both at airports and at town terminals. These exams consisted of written papers followed by an oral. The staff we were testing were clerical staff (i.e. non-management) who started on 'C' Scale and progressed by these tests through 'B' to 'A' Scale. The next step beyond was on to the 'M' (Management) Scales; this was obviously a stressful process for some but we, as Inspectors, did all we could to help staff through, and this even included offering Polo Mints to tearful ladies!

In the early days, BEA operated as far as Bahrain in the Gulf and their flight crews in this region were dressed in khaki uniforms, very similar to those worn by the RAF in the tropics. However, by the time I joined the airline, its longhaul operations were restricted to linking London with Cyprus, Tel Aviv, Beirut and Istanbul. Every day a BEA Comet left Heathrow for the Eastern Mediterranean, stopping *en route* at Rome and Athens. From Athens the aircraft would operate alternately to each of the four destinations mentioned. On the days the flight did not operate to your particular destination, you were obliged to transfer to another flight in Athens.

For those not familiar with the Comet 4, I must explain that, although it was a beautiful aircraft and very popular with passengers, it had one serious deficiency. The belly holds in which baggage, cargo and mail had to be stowed were long and very shallow and the access to them was a small hatch at the base of the hold. Any use of pallets or mechanised loading was out of the question. There was one large hold aft of the passenger cabin which was easily accessible and could accommodate bulky items. The problem with this hold was that it was so far aft that if any great weight was placed in there, the aircraft's centre of gravity would fall outside its permissible Aft Limit.

The reason for explaining the complication of the Comet's Eastern Mediterranean operations and the loading difficulties is to show why the greatest problem I had to cope with as an Inspector was passengers arriving at their destination without their baggage.

Let us take, for example, a Comet leaving Heathrow for Rome, Athens and Beirut. The Load Control Clerk at Heathrow would not only have to ensure that the aircraft left within its weight limits with the correct fuel, but also had to give detailed instructions to the Loading staff as to where in the long narrow holds to load baggage, cargo and mail for Rome, Athens and Beirut. This had to be done in such a way that intermediate airports could gain access to their load whilst also ensuring that the centre of gravity of the aircraft remained within its C. of G. limits.

What I have described would have been simple if infinite time were available but, in reality, the Load Control Clerk only received his passenger and baggage weights a very short time before departure. He then had to assess how much cargo he could accommodate within the weight remaining. All these functions were common to all aircraft but proved particularly difficult with the Comet.

Let us assume that London had done well with the load for Beirut, placed at the end of the hold furthest from the entrance. Next would be the load for Athens, and lastly, the load for Rome. Thus, when the aircraft arrived in Rome, the load for that airport would be adjacent to the hold door. Rome now had to load baggage, cargo and mail for Athens and Beirut and the easiest option would be to place it in the area vacated by the load just removed. If this were done, the load for Athens put on by London would be further away from the hold entrance than the load for Beirut put on in Rome. Thus, when the aircraft arrived in Athens, the Beirut load would have to be taken off the aeroplane for Athens to gain access to its own load!

I am sorry to have laboured this point, but even if the reader remains confused, this reflects, to some degree, the last few minutes of an aircraft's departure preparation. The greatest emphasis was placed on the aircraft being safe but, in the last minute haste, correct distribution of load within the holds for the convenience of airports down the route, was, at times, not done correctly. The net result of all this was that some baggage was offloaded at an intermediate airport which should have stayed abroad, and *vice versa*.

In an endeavour to solve these loading problems, I was sent to Scandinavia by the BEA Traffic Manager to look at the SAS Traffic Dispatcher system. They were the only people in Europe at the time using Traffic Dispatchers. Their Traffic Dispatcher, distinguished by his red cap, co-ordinated all aspects of each flight departure and was responsible for the aircraft departing on schedule, correctly loaded and with correct documentation. He was always on site at the aircraft and provided a good link with the Captain. As a result of my report, BEA introduced Traffic Dispatchers at Heathrow and the Traffic Inspectors were tasked with training them.

To give an indication of the size of the mishandled baggage problem on this route, BEA employed two 'Security' staff at Rome who were occupied full-time on baggage tracing, i.e. locating mishandled baggage and restoring it to its owner as quickly as possible

The advent of the Trident onto the Mediterranean routes brought about a marked improvement. The holds were large, accessible and one could easily climb inside to sort things out. I must emphasise that BEA passengers were not alone in suffering mishandled baggage. The problem was so bad that IATA (the International Air Transport Association) had to introduce special procedures and held annual 'Baggage Weeks' to attempt to reduce the problem.

Let us now leave the Eastern Mediterranean and go south to Libya. The airport I had to inspect was Idris airport, named after the King. BEA operated a Viscount service from Rome through Malta to Tripoli. Conditions for passengers at Tripoli airport were generally well below acceptable standards, and the toilet facilities were appalling, lacking the main essential of water!

Whilst I was involved with Tripoli, King Idris was removed from power and the airport name changed. It became an offence to use the name 'Idris,' which proved particularly difficult for the Air Traffic Controllers who were accustomed to using their radio callsign 'Idris Tower.' A number of these Controllers were British and found it difficult to continue working for their new militantly Islamic masters. The Libyan airline was KLA, Kingdom of Libya Airlines, so almost overnight, all reference to 'Kingdom' had to be removed from aircraft and airline documents.

These strict new regulations, imposed by the Libyan authorities, also meant that, before the Viscount service left Malta for Tripoli, all reference to the Kingdom of Libya had to be removed from any publications carried on the aircraft. Also, any mention of the existence of the State of Israel was forbidden. This meant replacing all passenger information folders in the seat pockets with appropriately censored versions. Customs at Tripoli airport also strongly objected to items in passengers' baggage bearing the Marks & Spencer brand label. At worst, this could lead to threats of detaining the aircraft.

I shall now say a little of my initial encounter in the early 1960s with the Eastern Bloc, as it used to be described. My first visit was to inspect Moscow airport (then Sheremetievo). Because this was a duty visit, I had to go as a guest of Aeroflot and my accommodation was arranged by the State Tourist Organisation, Intourist. I was given a room on the 16th floor of the Hotel Ukraine after surrendering my passport to the police with instructions to apply for its return on the day of my departure. This did not alleviate, in any way, the feeling I was already getting of not being particularly welcome.

The BEA representative in Moscow was a very pleasant British engineer who looked after the airline's interests in Russia and supervised the handling provided by Aeroflot. BEA also employed two Russian staff in an attempt to add some western style of customer service for passengers. Aeroflot then was undoubtedly the largest airline in the world in terms of its aircraft fleet and had a total monopoly of ticket sales within Russia, and therefore had no real incentive to give a good passenger service.

It was interesting to speak with the local staff. One of them told me with complete confidence that within a few years Russia would rule the world and that while he was waiting for this great event he was quite content to assist BEA! I was shown all round the airport, which was strictly functional and largely military. What did surprise me was that there was no objection to my filming military aircraft.

On my first night in Moscow, the BEA representative invited me to his apartment for dinner, where I learned sufficient about the difficulties of working and living in Moscow to decide never to accept a posting there. After a pleasant evening, I found a taxi which I had to share with a drunken American who, to my embarrassment, started to tell the driver "what he could do with Moscow"! I rather hoped that the taxi driver would have a very limited grasp of English as I wished to arrive intact at my hotel. The driver showed no signs of having understood the tirade of abuse against his fatherland but, when I arrived at the hotel, he said in perfect English and without a trace of emotion: "You Americans have no culture"!

Having reached the hotel, I thought my problems were over as it was now well after midnight and I was looking forward to a good night's sleep. Not so; having reached the 16th floor of the hotel in a very ponderous lift, I asked for my room key. All the keys for each floor were hung on a wall behind a desk, at which sat their custodian. The custodian of the keys on my floor was a formidable woman (of the body-building type) who appeared to speak no English and, although it was obvious from my pointing to the keys that I wished access to my room, I got no response except for a general indication that she was not about to grant my wish. As diplomatically as I could I persuaded her to find somebody capable of speaking English who could act as an arbitrator in this absurd impasse. After what seemed an age, she spoke to somebody on the phone and then handed me the receiver. The man at the other end did not exude customer benevolence, but at least we could communicate. He explained that I could not be given my key because I had not paid my bill. I then explained that I had only just arrived and, after a long silence, I was told to hand the phone back to my 'key lady.' Without a glimmer of a smile or any sign of apology, she gave me the key.

In my room at last – a bit Spartan, but at least I could have a bath – I then discovered that there was no bath plug and, when I checked the hand basin, I found that this was similarly bereft. At this stage I had become determined to beat the system, and sat in the bath with my heel in the plughole. I have yet to discover what one is meant to do. Perhaps Russians carry their own plugs?

On the next morning I went downstairs looking forward to a good breakfast and, having allowed ample time before being picked up by the BEA car, I sat down and waited . . . and waited. Eventually somebody took my order and I waited, again, hopefully. Finally, right on time, the BEA car arrived, but my elusive breakfast did not. On subsequent mornings I abandoned any hope of breakfast.

My next encounter with the Eastern Bloc was Warsaw, where I found the people much more friendly than in Moscow, but I was appalled by the lack of food in the shops and the length of the queues of the people waiting for what supplies were available.

Whilst in Warsaw most of my dealings were with the national airline, LOT, who handled our flights. Their management staff were easy to talk to when you could find the individual you wanted. Any one individual never seemed to be available on two consecutive days. This, I later discovered, was because most people had two jobs to compensate for the low level of pay.

There was a noticeable warmth and friendliness in the Poles which had been markedly lacking in the Russians with whom I had dealings.

As a Traffic Inspector, some of my happiest times were in Scotland when, apart from dealing with the relatively large airports at Prestwick, Glasgow (Renfrew at this time) and Edinburgh (Turnhouse), I also visited the little airports in the Highlands and Islands, which were fascinating and did things in their own way.

Initially, I was viewed with some suspicion as a foreigner coming up from London to tell the Scots how to do their job. Fortunately, their barrier soon broke down as we got to know each other and they discovered I might even be able to assist them.

The large Scottish airports at Edinburgh and Glasgow were served by frequent Vickers Vanguard flights from Heathrow. This aircraft was ideal for shorthaul flights in that it was very easy to load and could therefore be turned round quickly at airports, thus giving excellent utilisation. From a passenger point of view, it was rather cramped, having up to 139 seats packed into it. Another drawback of the Vanguard was that the entire fuselage had a tendency to vibrate, which made long journeys rather wearisome, e.g. London to Malta.

Within Scotland, BEA operated an interesting assortment of aircraft to cope with the particular needs of the area and the primitive airports into which the airline was flying. An added responsibility undertaken by BEA in Scotland was to provide an Air Ambulance Service. The aircraft used for this service was the piston-engined de Havilland Heron which was based at Renfrew. There were originally three Herons in service, but in 1957 a Heron answering an emergency call to Islay crashed in terrible weather conditions killing the two pilots and the nurse.

Of the remaining Herons, one would be kept on standby for emergency calls while the other, with 14 passenger seats, operated scheduled services to places such as Tiree and Barra. Barra, in the Outer Hebrides, is the most unusual commercial airfield I have ever visited. The only runway is the beach and the schedules in the BEA timetables were shown as being 'subject to tide.'

The Station Superintendent at Barra was a lady, Kitty McPherson, who used to be driven from home to the airport by the rest of the BEA station staff – one man, who drove the fire appliance and coped with loading the aircraft. The terminal building on the beach was a large shed divided into two parts, one half being the BEA office and the other the passenger lounge. Passengers could brew their own tea or coffee from what was provided and were trusted to place the appropriate money in a tin according to a price list hanging on the wall.

The aircraft arrival procedures at Barra were as follows. The Heron from Glasgow would fly to Tiree; then, if the weather seemed favourable, it would continue to overhead Barra. The Station Superintendent carried a portable VHF radio with which to speak to the Captain and advise him whether or not the beach was fit for landing. This was a highly technical decision based largely on how far the seagulls feet sank into the sand!

Apart from the Herons, BEA in Scotland operated Vickers Viscounts and Handley Page Heralds. Airports within Scotland which I had to visit, and have not yet mentioned, were Aberdeen, Inverness, Benbecula,

Stornoway, Wick, Orkney, Shetland and Campbeltown, the latter having the largest runway in Scotland as it was built for NATO emergency use. The interesting thing about these small Scottish airports was that they served a community where everybody knew each other, which sometimes made the enforcement of BEA's regulations difficult.

There was a case where it was found that the Station Superintendent was operating his own commercial business from the BEA premises, with the result that BEA revenue was declining. He admitted his guilt and was dismissed; he then set up a travel agency in the same town and, because he was a man of influence, he drew to his agency the ticket sales that would previously have gone to the BEA office. (I am told that his influence came from his having a hold on the local fishing rights!) In the end, BEA was paying commission to the man they had sacked.

I recall another interesting happening. Because these small aircraft only had a few seats, there were times when demand greatly exceeded supply. On one such occasion, a local dignitary had been unable to obtain a seat at the Sales Office. Shortly after, on the Station Superintendent's office desk there arrived a huge salmon with a note from the dignitary saying: "I shall be on Friday's flight from Glasgow." I rather suspect some less eminent citizen may have lost his seat.

One of the other fascinating aspects of aviation in Scotland was the spirit of co-operation between all parties. In Kirkwall, for example, the southbound aircraft used to pick up a large consignment of lobsters. I have seen the refuelling company staff, ATC, and airport management staff helping in the loading of the aircraft when the flight was running late. The reason was very simple – the sooner the flight departed, the sooner they could all go home.

I mentioned earlier that one of my special projects was the introduction into BEA of the Trident 1. This involved writing instructions on the ground handling of the aircraft at all airports to which the Trident would operate, or to which it might divert. It was then necessary to visit most of these places with the aircraft when it landed there on proving flights; this was luxury travel indeed as I was often the only person in the aircraft cabin and naturally used the First Class accommodation. Flying on proving flights was great fun, but exhausting. Unlike the flight crew I had no statutory limits on my duty time. On one day I flew from London to Helsinki and back, London to Madrid and back, and then London to Athens and back. At each airport I had to meet with the local Airport Authority staff and handling agents to explain the particular requirements of the Trident.

From the ground handling point of view, the Trident posed two unusual problems. Firstly, the nose undercarriage was offset to port, which meant that most of the passenger steps in use at foreign airports could not be positioned at the forward passenger door because they fouled the undercarriage. This necessitated BEA supplying special steps or paying for local ones to be modified. The second problem was that the Trident 1 had an auxiliary power unit (APU) situated in the belly of the aircraft with the jet efflux aimed straight at the ground.

The Trident I APU caused great difficulties with Airport Authorities, because not only was it extremely noisy, it was also liable to damage any surface on which it was parked. Some airport aprons (aircraft parking areas) had lighting built into the apron surface. The efflux from the APU had the habit of destroying these lights and also melting the rubberised joint sealing between the concrete blocks, of which the aprons were built. To overcome these problems, BEA designed a large wheel-mounted engine noise muffler, one end of which was positioned under the aircraft where the jet blast emerged, whilst at the other end, the blast was deflected upwards. The contraption had the desired effect, but increased the congestion around the rear hold and added greatly to the cost of introducing the Trident. These cumbersome APU mufflers had to be sent to all airports to which the Trident operated. When the Trident diverted to a non-scheduled airport where there was no muffler, the Airport Authorities used to insist on the aircraft being parked in some remote part of the airfield well clear of the passenger terminal. The APU in later versions of the Trident were located in the tail of the aircraft.

The Trident was equipped with passenger seats specially designed for BEA which permitted rapid configuration changes to match the ratio of First-Tourist Class seats to the demand. The Trident passenger cabin had three compartments; the two smaller compartments forward of the wing could each have eight First Class passengers or twelve Tourist Class. To change a row of three seats from First Class to Tourist was simple: the armrests separating the centre seat from the outer two were moved towards each other and formed the base of a drinks table. Thus, the two outer seats assumed the width of First Class seats. The seats were already in Pullman arrangement around a centre table and had adequate legroom for First Class. According to demand, the Trident 1 could be operated with 16F/54T, 8F/76T or 88T.

Because of my experience with Trident introduction into BEA I was sent on loan to Kuwait Airways when they purchased a fleet of Trident IE aircraft. My visit to Kuwait had rather an inauspicious start: because I was going back to a hot country, I decided to travel in a tropical suit I used to wear when with BOAC. I was given a First Class ticket by Kuwait Airways to travel on their Comet service via Beirut to Kuwait. All went normally until, as I eased myself into a window seat, I heard a terrible tearing noise. The suit had obviously been out of action too long and the seam at the seat of my trousers had parted over too great a length to retain any decency or dignity. All my other clothes were inaccessible in the hold so I sat for some time contemplating how to extricate myself from this dilemma. I asked the stewardess for as many safety pins as she could lay her hands on and, waiting until my fellow passengers were immersed in their pre-dinner drinks, I reversed rapidly down the cabin to take refuge in the toilet. There I effected a very creditable repair job which, I am thankful to say, held until I could change in my hotel room in Kuwait.

Thereafter, my stay in Kuwait was entirely satisfactory and I was very well looked after by my hosts, Kuwait Airways. However, on return to England I was asked by HM Customs in Terminal 3 what I had obtained whilst abroad. I showed them various gifts which did not interest them but they came upon a box of 35 mm transparencies. I explained that these only depicted various aspects of the Trident but I was detained while they satisfied themselves they were not pornographic slides from the Middle East. There were, at that time, a lot of dubious photographs being marketed in that part of the world. In the event, Customs must have found my slides most uninteresting and I was soon on my way.

Whilst I was a Traffic Inspector with BEA I was sent in an emergency to take over the post of Airline Representative in Prague. The incumbent had become seriously ill and was undergoing surgery in a local hospital. The man was too ill to give me any sort of handover but I did see him briefly in the hospital and spoke with the surgeon. By British standards the hospital was pretty basic and cheerless and the surgeon came to see me in a white but very bloodstained coat, in which he looked more like a butcher. However, he had obviously done a good job and my colleague was flown back to England to convalesce.

Prague is a beautiful city and I was accommodated in an enormous house allocated to foreigners by some government department. I was told that these houses allocated to foreigners had originally belonged to the aristocracy and had been commandeered by the Communists when they came into power.

There were effectively three types of currency in use in Prague. There was the ordinary money in which nationals were paid and a special currency only available to foreigners in exchange for hard currency; this special currency could be used to purchase Western goods not available to the ordinary Czechoslovakian. In addition to these two currencies were packets of Western cigarettes. You could, for example, negotiate the price of a purchase in terms of packets of Rothmans.

Working in Prague was both fascinating and aggravating. The local people were obviously not encouraged to fraternise with foreigners, though I got the impression that most of them would like to have done so. In the office, my senior Czechoslovakian staff member openly admitted he had to keep an eye on what I was doing and report regularly to some government official on my activities. I had a company car but was restricted to driving within a certain range of the city. I was assured that, if I strayed beyond my limits, the police would know this from the car's registration plates.

Because one could not socialise with the locals one's entire social life was centred on the numerous Embassy parties. This was very pleasant to begin with but after a while you kept meeting the same people irrespective of which Embassy was giving the party.

I would very much like to revisit this city now that it has a more enlightened government. Even under the Communists it was a strikingly beautiful place.

After holding the fort in Prague, I returned to Heathrow and further involvement with the Trident. The Trident was at the forefront of what we now take for granted – All Weather Operations – or, in layman's terms, the ability to land an aircraft in fog. BEA introduced the 'Autoland' system with the advent of the Trident 1; it was a British-designed system enabling pilots to do 'hands off' landings in zero visibility. After extensive trials without passengers, the Trident was cleared by the Ministry of Aviation to 'Autoland' with passengers, and this first occurred on a Trident flight from Paris on June 10th 1965.

I will deal with the more technical aspects of All Weather Operations but the reasons for their development were mainly commercial. BEA, for profitability, had to attract and retain business traffic: these passengers paid full fares and often travelled First Class. BEA reasoned that, after safety, the things businessmen most required from an airline were punctuality and reliability. The hub of BEA's operations was Heathrow and therefore at the mercy of British weather. Research into BEA's operations showed that between 1964 and 1969, bad weather accounted for 86% of diversions, 37% of cancelled flights and 27% of flights arriving over one hour late. Thus BEA estimated that, with the introduction of the Trident with 'Autoland,' they would gain a considerable advantage over their competitors operating into and out of Heathrow – and they proved correct.

With the Trident, BEA also introduced in Europe seat allocation at check-in on multi- and single-sector flights. Seat allocation we now take for granted but, prior to its introduction, there was liable to be an unseemly rush across the apron to the aircraft with the most agile gaining the best seats whilst mothers with children came last – I was given the task of devising the scheme.

On the commercial front, BEA scored another 'first' when, in 1965, the 'Beacon' computer system was introduced. In essence, this was a computerised reservations system based in the West London Air Terminal. This avoided the need for staff to scrutinise long sheets of paper any time somebody wanted to book a seat – they merely called up the appropriate flight on the computer screen. The introduction of 'Beacon' gave BEA a great advantage in the UK in that it could give superior service to Travel Agents and individual callers. The next stage was to connect some 22 overseas stations to 'Beacon' (via landlines, multiplexers, modems, etc.); this brought BEA a huge advantage over their competitors in Europe.

Prior to the remoting of 'Beacon' to outstations, making a reservation from a foreign BEA sales office was not a simple process. Let us take, for example, a prospective passenger walking into the BEA office in Istanbul and wishing to arrange a business trip to London, Manchester and New York on BEA/BOAC. The sales assistant in the Istanbul office could probably confirm a seat for the passenger on the Istanbul/London sector but would have to signal London for confirmation of the London/-Manchester sector and the Manchester/New York on the BOAC flight, which used to operate Manchester/Prestwick/New York. Confirmation from London could take days to arrive, by which time BEA might well have lost the business to an airline which could provide a slicker service. After the provision of access to 'Beacon' at remote stations, confirmation of bookings could be given almost instantaneously.

During my time with BEA I was privileged to be placed in charge of two of the largest stations outside London – Manchester and Rome airports. I was only in post as Station Manager in Manchester for some two months during an interregnum, but sufficient time to meet a lot of interesting people, both customers and staff.

The highlight of my BEA career was when I was given a permanent posting to Rome as Senior Traffic Officer, and later as a Station Manager. BEA in Rome was a large organisation where, apart from handling its own flights, it also undertook handling for BOAC, QANTAS, Malta Airlines, Air Ceylon, Nigeria Airways, South African Airways, East African Airways, Central African Airways, Cyprus Airways and various British charter operators.

The airport in Rome where BEA operated was Fiumicino, which had been built largely on land reclaimed from the sea and swamp and was renowned for its mosquito population. The second, and older, airport serving Rome was Ciampino and this was still the diversion alternate for Fiumicino. I spent many night hours at Ciampino when fog descended on the swamp-based Fiumicino.

There were two reasons for putting Rome at the top of my BEA career. Firstly, it is a beautiful place to live, both from a scenery and climate point of view. I had my wife and two young daughters with me living in a fabulous villa in the country and near the coast. Secondly the job itself was challenging and interesting – much time doing battle with the Airport Authority! – and, above all, I found the Italian staff wonderful. They were so loyal and friendly to this young Englishman sent from London as their boss.

One characteristic of the Italians that impressed me was that they never seemed to worry about a problem until disaster struck. On more than one occasion, I had staff members in my office in tears because the bailiff was at that very moment taking the furniture from their apartment. The tears, which they seemed to be able to turn on at will to soften the heart of the English boss, were shed to obtain an immediate cash advance to resolve the current crisis. It usually succeeded – I always felt rather uncomfortable with weeping men in the office.

Other characteristics of the Italians which I appreciated were their cheerfulness, their hospitality and, above all, a great capacity for enjoying life for the present without undue concern about the future.

There were numerous entertaining incidents I could recall from my days in Rome, but I will restrict myself to just two.

At a particular time when the Italian Government had imposed a total prohibition on animal imports, BEA at Rome airport became host to an elephant. The young elephant had travelled in a crate from Nairobi on a BOAC Boeing 707. The animal had been stowed in a belly hold but had obviously arched its back, broken the crate and damaged the aircraft floor. The BOAC Captain refused to carry the elephant on to London, its destination, so we offloaded the animal. The authorities were adamant that we could not bring the beast into Italy so we had to clear out an airside cargo office for use as an elephant house pending the arrival, a few days later, of an Argosy freighter which could accommodate our guest. Our cargo staff seemed quite happy to feed the animal but were not so keen on the necessary cleaning.

One evening I was on the apron watching the handling of a BOAC VC.10 in transit from London to Nairobi and Johannesburg. The baggage for

Rome had been unloaded and was being towed on a train of baggage trucks to the terminal. One of our baggage handling staff was driving the little Mercury tractor pulling the trucks. The tractor was equipped with a canvas hood for weather protection and at sunset it was fairly dark inside the cab. Suddenly I saw the baggage train stopped abruptly and the driver fled from the cab shouting: "Il Diablo, Il Diablo!"

When calmed down a little, he said he had seen the devil behind him in the cab. He was usually a rational fellow so we investigated. Peering into the cab we saw what our driver had seen – two large white eyes and a mass of teeth. They belonged to an African passenger from the BOAC flight who was being deported from London back to Kenya. He had tried to escape deportation by hiding behind the driver's seat until the flight had departed!

All good things come to an end, and I was brought back to England on promotion to become Sales Services Superintendent for the Mediterranean Region of the airline. This was really a marketing job involving a lot of travel, but it had taken me away from aviation to commerce. I was not in my element: much of my time was to be spent in a headquarters' office and at meetings. I had to get back to the frontline with aeroplanes and passengers.

TOP: Dragon Rapide G-AEWL, the aircraft in which the author had his first flight at Ramsgate in 1951.
BOTTOM: The author preparing to fly Tiger Moth G-AMVX at Panshanger during 1955.

Other types flown by the author included:
TOP: Chipmunk G-AORK, "Klondike Kate," at Fair Oaks during 1955.
BOTTOM: Provost T.1 at Syerston, 1956.

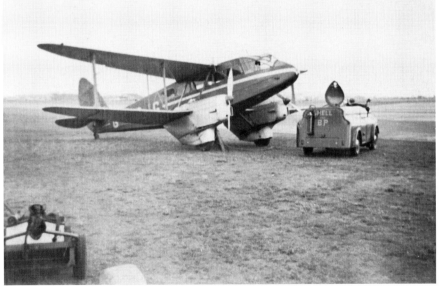

TOP: The original Heathrow Control Tower on the North Side of the airport, with a BOAC Argonaut taxying by.
BOTTOM: Throughout the early days of Heathrow, pleasure flights were available in several Dragon Rapides of Island Airways including G-AGJG (which is currently being restored to flying condition).

The participants in a BOAC Station Officers' course in 1958 pose in front of one of the Company's Stratocruisers ("Cambria", G-AKGJ); the author is 3rd from left in back row.

TOP: Entry to the Central Area Tunnel as it used to be.
BOTTOM: The main concourse of Terminal 2 in the early 1960s.

TOP: The Herald was used on Scotland's internal routes.
BOTTOM: A reflective shot of BEA Trident 1C (G-ARPB) at Heathrow.

TOP: The Avro York G-ANTK (referred to in Chapter 2), now under restoration at Duxford.
BOTTOM: The Airport Duty Manager's means of airside transport is dwarfed by a Japan Airlines B.747 (mid-1980s).

TOP: The Senior Traffic Officer (author) in his BEA office at Fiumicino airport (Rome) in 1967.
BOTTOM: BEA staff at Rome receive a Certificate of Commendation from BOAC, 1967 (the author on extreme right).

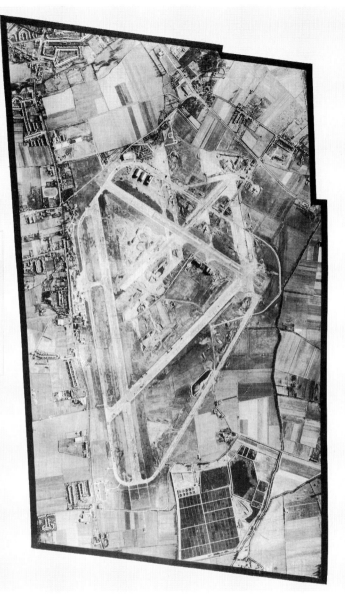

LONDON AIRPORT, HEATHROW, MIDDLESEX
IN COURSE OF CONSTRUCTION. 16/1/47

An aerial view of Heathrow in about 1970; the Northern Apron was still in

An aerial view of the Central Area stands – before the building of Eurolounge.

The Heathrow Control Tower in the mid-seventies.

CHAPTER FOUR

BRITISH AIRPORTS AUTHORITY (1970)

If the reader's patience is exceptional and he is still with me, I shall now talk about Heathrow – the object of the exercise. The previous chapters were only to show that, when I came to Heathrow, I did have some experience of aviation on which to form my opinions of this great airport.

In early 1970, whilst perusing budgets and sales results in my office in BEA Headquarters in Ruislip, I became convinced that I had been divorced from aircraft and real aviation and was determined to do something to rectify the situation. As in the past, I never do anything in a straightforward manner. I knew the Airport Chaplain and asked him if he knew of any interesting jobs with the British Airports Authority; this query resulted in my having a pub lunch with the BAA Non-Industrial Personnel Officer (now a retired BAA Board Member). Sometime later I was again sitting uninspired in my office when I had a phone call from the Heathrow Operations chief asking me to come and see him. We met in his office and I was offered a post as an Operations Officer – not only did the content of the job appeal to me but I was told that the BAA would pay the cost of maintaining my pilot's licence!

The Heathrow airport and its management that I joined on the 1st June 1970 were very different from those I left 23 years later. The man in overall charge was the General Manager, "Wally" Waldron, and reporting to him were Deputy General Managers. My boss was Deputy General Manager

(Operations), George Warcup, and he was responsible for everything connected with the safe operation of aircraft in and out of Heathrow. Rather surprisingly, he was also in charge of the Airport Police with the Chief Constable of the BAA Constabulary reporting to him.

George Warcup, who sadly died very suddenly a year or so after I joined the BAA, was a great man in every sense. He was a man of immense aviation experience and had, at one time, been Airport Commandant at Heathrow, and this title remained displayed above his office door even in the BAA days. He still occupied the Commandant's House on the north side of the airport and retained the shooting rights on the airfield and was to be seen at times on the airfield with his 12-bore.

Under the D/General Manager (Operations) were a Senior Operations Manager, a Station Operations Officer and four Operations Officers; without exception, all of these were pilots or navigators from the armed forces or the airlines so I had joined a group I could easily settle in with. The rest of the BAA environment I found more difficult to adapt to, as it was so very 'Ministry' in outlook and practice. To label the early BAA management as 'Ministry' is perhaps rather unfair, but never having been a civil servant myself I found their ways different. In the airline environment the use of first names was common between staff of differing grades but, in the then BAA, titles seemed all-important, as did the size of your office and its carpet – if your grade entitled you to one! The reason for this strong Ministry bias is not surprising: Heathrow had been owned and staffed by The Ministry of Aviation and Civil Aviation Ministries (various titles) until taken over on the 1st April 1966 by the newly-created British Airports Authority. Most of the staff of the BAA initially came from the Ministry.

I am no historian and this book does not set out to be a history of Heathrow, which has already been well documented, but a few words about its origin seem apt . . .

In its June issue of 1944, *"The Aeroplane"* magazine reported: "The London airport has been sited just off the Great West Road between East Bedfont and Stanwell. The minimum official requirements were a flat piece of open country sufficiently large to cope with future air traffic and situated as close to the metropolitan centre as possible with good road and rail connections. In the centre of the area is a sewage farm of the Middlesex County Council which will have to be removed. The Underground railway runs as far as Hounslow West, which could be extended to serve the new airport itself."

It is interesting to note the reference to the sewage works and the Underground. Since its first flight on New Year's Day in 1946, the airport and the sewage works have co-existed happily (provided the wind is in the right direction!) and it is only now, with the planning for Terminal 5, that moves are in hand to resite the sewage works. A small point of interest is that the last reported sighting of a wolf in the wild in England was in the Heathrow Perry Oaks sewage works.

The connecting of the Underground to Heathrow, although obviously a good idea, did not take place until many years later. One of my early tasks as an Operations Officer was to decide where the ventilation shafts connecting the Underground tunnel to the surface could be sited without infringing Runway and Taxiway clearances (safe areas each side to protect aircraft).

In 1944 the Air Ministry, using wartime emergency powers, acquired an area of 2,800 acres, including most of Heathrow village and Richard Fairey's Great West Aerodrome.

The honour of operating the first passenger flight out of Heathrow went to Air Vice Marshal Donald Bennett. He was piloting a Lancastrian developed from the Lancaster bomber and not dissimilar to the Avro York mentioned earlier in this book. The aircraft belonged to British South American Airlines and carried ten passengers to Buenos Aires via Portugal, West Africa, Brazil and Uruguay.

It is a great credit to the wisdom and foresight of those who built and planned the runways and taxiways of Heathrow that they are now able to cope with over 1,000 aircraft movements per day and with aircraft the size of the Boeing 747, which could never have been imagined.

Originally, Heathrow was to have three runways in the traditional service aerodrome triangular pattern, the main runway being adjacent to the Bath Road (now referred to as 27R/09L). The longer-term plan envisaged nine runways. An additional runway was to be built parallel to each of the original ones, thus forming a "Star of David" pattern. Another triangular pattern of three runways was planned to be built north of the Bath Road with the road itself passing through a tunnel. Because of the prevalence of flying boats at this period, there were also plans to incorporate a water runway at Heathrow for their use!

When I started duties at Heathrow as an Operations Officer three runways remained – two parallel runways, 28R/10L and 28L/10R (two figures such as '28' show the magnetic bearing of the runways – e.g. the magnetic bearing of runway 28 is 280 degrees magnetic. The suffix 'R' or 'L' is added to distinguish between right and left when parallel runways exist).

With the change of magnetic variation, runways designated 28/10 have now changed to 27/09. The third runway was 23/05, a shorter runway orientated north-east/south-west. This is the runway arrangement still in use as I write, except that both the parallel runways have been extended to the west to accommodate heavier aircraft requiring longer take-off runs.

The original runways were built with concrete blocks, the paved area being 300 ft wide. In recent years the runways have been given a new asphalt surface which not only provides improved friction characteristics essential for aircraft but, because of its porous surface, prevents rainwater accumulating on the runway.

The resurfacing of the runways was a major operation, which had to be carried out during the night so that the runway could be back in use during the day. It was not simply a matter of laying tarmac; each runway is covered in light fittings with their associated transformers, ducts and access pits, all of which need raising or rebuilding. After a night's work on the runway, it had to be most carefully inspected by the Operations Officer and his Ground Operations staff before he returned it to ATC for use by aircraft. The difficulty with resurfacing a long runway is that you can only complete a certain length each night. The completed section is then considerably higher than the original and a temporary tarmac ramp has to be built at the end of each night's work to enable aircraft to pass from one level to the other. Many complaints came from BEA Trident pilots because these ramps apparently caused serious oscillation in the pitching plane to occur on take off. Another difficulty was that these temporary ramps could start to break up after heavy use. A Ground Operations staff member was detailed to keep a constant watch on the ramps through binoculars. On a fine sunny day this was a popular task as it entailed sitting in a deck chair on the grass opposite the ramp.

The two main runways at Heathrow, 27R and 27L are 12,800 ft and 12,000 ft in length respectively, while the crosswind runway (23) is 8,000 ft. The two main runways are Category 3 in each direction; this means that they comply with all the requirements in terms of Instrument Landing System and runway lighting, and safeguarding for landings in very low visibility to be carried out by aircraft appropriately equipped.

I mentioned earlier that I was involved with the introduction of the Trident in BEA. When I joined the BAA, I was immediately involved in the establishment at Heathrow of all the ground facilities for Category 3 operations by the Trident which was, at the time, the only aircraft so equipped.

The landing of the aircraft in low visibility required primarily a very accurate Instrument Landing System. The Civil Aviation Authority installed new Plessey ILS Localisers and Glidepaths (Stan 37 and 38). In simple terms, the ILS system radiates two radio beams to guide an incoming aircraft. The aircraft lines up with the centreline of the correct runway by following the beam transmitted by the Localiser aerial and descends at the right angle and on the correct path by following the beam from the Glidepath aerial. An aircraft autopilot can lock onto these beams and follow them down to a predetermined height above the ground, at which point the human pilot takes over to carry out the landing. An ordinary autopilot cannot be allowed to continue to the actual landing because, being electro-mechanical, it could be subject to failure with catastrophic results.

In order to enable the Trident to land automatically, it was equipped with a Triplex Flight system. In essence, this consisted of three computerized autopilots designed to operate independently, locking onto the ILS and passing signals to servo-amplifiers which, in turn, produced the required movement in the aircraft's control surfaces. In the unlikely event of one autopilot malfunctioning, it would be overridden by the other two.

The new ILS was so accurate and sensitive that precautions had to be taken on the airfield to prevent the beam being distorted by aircraft or vehicles coming too close to it. Runway Holding Points, the positions at which aircraft wait prior to entering the runway for take-off, had to be moved further from the runway for low visibility operations and Operations staff had to patrol the airfield to ensure no vehicles infringed the ILS restricted areas.

The ILS beam is constantly checked on the ground by Field Monitors, aerials which ensure the beam is within its limits and shut down the system should it not be so. In the early days of CAT 3 operations, we used to have problems with birds, particularly a sparrowhawk, which insisted on sitting on these aerials and tripping the system!

Apart from the ILS requirements for low visibility operations, runway and taxiway lighting had to be uprated to high intensity and supplementary approach and touchdown zone lighting had to be installed.

Another requirement for low visibility operations is that there should never be a power supply failure of more than one second to the approach and runway lighting. At Heathrow, this was achieved by having an essential services ring main which could be supplied by any of three independent electricity generating stations. In addition, there are diesel generators on the airfield which can be brought into operation to supply airfield lighting.

Also essential for low visibility operations is the provision of an accurate measurement of Runway Visual Range (RVR) to enable the pilot to assess whether to attempt a landing. RVR used to be assessed by human observers by seeing how far down the runway they could see lights or marker boards, but with the advent of CAT 3 operations a more sophisticated system was needed. RVR measurement is now carried out automatically by devices called Transmissometers. Three of these devices are placed alongside the runway, at the touchdown point, mid-point and at the end, and they pass RVR readings to a display in the Control Tower. ATC then relay this to the pilot.

Each Transmissometer unit consists of two yellow 'Dalek'-like objects placed 10 metres apart. One of the two 'Daleks' transmits a beam of light to the other which reflects it back. The system then compares the intensity of the light at source with that of the reflected beam which has passed through the atmosphere and assesses the visibility.

I shall now leave the complexities of CAT 3 and return to Heathrow as I found it in the early 1970s. Airport Department heads did not keep their own budgets, this function being carried out by an Accounts Department at Hayes. However, soon the BAA decided that General Managers would take over their own budgets. Rather in character, my boss initially refused to do so on the grounds that the *status quo* was quite satisfactory! He was overruled and, turning to me at a particular meeting on the subject, he said: "I don't want the budget – you can do it!".

I was, at the time, the most junior of the Operations Officers so I was not in a position to protest. I remember trying to sort out whether items of expenditure were capital or revenue! I don't think I ever really understood budgets as they were then, but fortunately at that time, CAT 3 was in vogue and practically any expenditure was approved if placed under the heading of CAT 3. That said, I was in danger, again, of becoming office-bound and remote from aircraft and passengers.

I was saved by the creation, in 1972, of the new post of Duty Operations Officer (DOO). This job was a shift-working post based alongside ATC in the Control Tower and responsible for all aspects of safe operation of the airfield. This included such things as: planning works on the field in such a way that ATC were not unduly restricted and no risk was encountered by aircraft or workers; co-ordination of aircraft emergencies; approach, runway and taxiway safeguarding; co-ordination of snow clearing; bird dispersal; investigating reports of objects falling from aircraft; and supervising the activities of the Marshalling, Ground Operations, Motor Transport and Apron Control sections.

I was one of the first six DOOs to be appointed and was delighted to be back on the front-line with much of my time spent on the airfield. On the airfield we always had radios tuned to one of the ATC frequencies but the VHF sets themselves were then large and comparatively unreliable. To change frequency you had to physically remove one crystal and insert another!

Before the creation of the DOO there was little management coverage outside office hours so one of us was always on standby at home for emergencies, and particularly for snow. Apart from mass industrial action, snow is potentially one of the most disruptive things to afflict an airport. The great difficulty for an Operations Officer is to have on hand the correct number of staff at the airport to cope with the snowfall. If he brings in too many staff and little snow falls, he has wasted a lot of money in overtime pay. If he has too few staff and a heavy fall comes, he is castigated by all the airlines for delays in clearing – being a Snow Co-ordinator (always an Operations Officer) can be a thankless task.

In the days before DOOs, as an Operations Officer you could be woken in the middle of the night in your home by the airport telephone exchange advising you that the Met. Office had issued a snow warning for Heathrow. You then had to call the Local Forecaster at the Heathrow Met. Office and, based on his advice and your own hunch (occasionally better), decide whether to bring in extra staff and, if necessary, go into the airport yourself. In any event, your sleep and that of your family was ruined. You were then, an hour or so later, woken again to be told that the snow warning had been cancelled!

Christmas Day 1970 was my first introduction to snow-clearing at Heathrow and also provided one of my more embarrassing moments. We swept snow all that day and through the night. In blizzard conditions and in the dark I, as the Operations Officer, agreed with ATC to close one of the main runways and led my convoy of snow-sweeping vehicles to the runway threshold. Having checked with ATC via R/T(radio), we entered the runway and, with the sweeping vehicles in echelon formation, we started clearing the runway.

The snow-clearing vehicles consisted of heavy lorries fitted with snow ploughs in the front and pulling specially-designed trailers on which were mounted 16 ft-wide cylindrical wire brushes powered by huge Packard engines. These vehicles were not, in those days, fitted with radio and therefore had to be escorted on the airfield by me, the Operations Officer, in a radio-equipped vehicle.

After some 90 minutes, I was congratulating myself on having achieved a good sweep, inspected the runway and returned it to ATC. I then set off back to Snow Base (a base set upon snow conditions as a centre of snow-clearing operations – usually an aircraft stand) with my eight snow vehicles following, or so I thought. I arrived safely at Snow Base and found, to my horror, I was on my own. Somewhere out there, in the dark, were eight huge vehicles. The only thing to do was to advise ATC to keep aircraft clear of the area we had been operating in until these vehicles had been located. On returning to the runway I discovered what had happened. Because of deep snow on the taxiways, it was impossible to see where the concrete stopped and the grass began. I had inadvertently turned off the taxiway onto the grass and, having a fairly light vehicle, had not noticed. The heavy vehicles following had sunk in the mud!

This incident did little for my ego, but I was encouraged later the same night when a very experienced Ops. Officer tried to clear a mound of snow by driving through it. He had not remembered there were concrete blocks in that part of the airfield, and parted company with the car's sump!

Although snow was very disruptive to one's social life and to the operation of the airport, I really enjoyed working in snow. There was a tremendous spirit of co-operation between Operations Officers and the MT staff who actually did the snow-clearing. Some of my best friendships started in blizzards! My boss would invariably appear to encourage the troops with words and a nip of Scotch from the bottle he usually produced on these occasions.

I can only remember one occasion when Heathrow was closed because of snow. Having two main runways enabled one to be used while the other was taken out of service for clearing.

To give some idea of the size of the task of clearing Heathrow of snow, the following facts must be considered. The main runways are approximately 2½ miles long and 100 yards wide; there are some 150 aircraft stands; there are miles of taxiways; there are thousands of lights to clear; all the airport roads, terminal forecourts and car parks etc. The most difficult problem the English weather can throw at Heathrow is a snowfall followed by a thaw and then a heavy frost – the result is ice, which is impossible to sweep. On occasions when Heathrow has been criticised for inefficient snow clearance, ice has usually been the problem.

Enough of snow! One of my special tasks was to rewrite Heathrow's Emergency Orders and to be responsible for their correct implementation. This meant that, when there was an aircraft emergency, I should be present. However, in those days, we only had one car for use on the airfield and it was usually elsewhere when I needed it. This provided me with a great opportunity. As I explained before, my boss was also in charge of the Airport Police and I knew they had Norton motorcycles. I wrote a note to my boss explaining my problem and asking that I be allocated a Police Norton. To my surprise he agreed and I soon acquired my bike. I was even provided with a helmet, appropriately painted yellow for the airfield! Thus, in my first year in the BAA, I had achieved a motorcycle to ride on duty and I was having my flying financed by the company. This was too good to last, and it did not.

When I became a Duty Operation Officer I had a fully-equipped Land Rover entirely at my disposal, so my reason for having the bike vanished; it was good while it lasted and I still use some of the police motorcycle clothing I was issued with.

The next disaster to strike was losing flying pay. There were, in the early 1970s, very few ladies in operational jobs but there were a number in administrative posts. One such lady in Head Office Personnel wrote to the

Operations Officers to say that "the BAA is not in the aviation business" and therefore our flying pay was to be discontinued (possibly an example of feminine logic!) In spite of our efforts through the Union and threats of court action, we lost out. I am still sure that had there not been so few of us and we had belonged to a strong Trade Union, the company would not have got away with it.

In those days, all staff were categorised Non-Industrial or Industrial. Staff such as porters were termed Industrial and were represented by the Transport and General Workers Union, which was strong at Heathrow. This resulted in management being over-cautious in their dealings with Industrial staff, which brought problems later to the efficient operation of the airport. For example, some staff obtained such favourable conditions that they became of little benefit to the company. This, in later years, was all sorted out, but it was a painful process.

I have concentrated, so far, on the operations aspects of Heathrow when I first joined the BAA. Now I think the Terminals deserve some attention. They were the responsibility of the Deputy General Manager (Traffic) and each had a Terminal Manager and Deputy Terminal Manager. On a 24-hour basis the terminals were staffed by Terminal Foremen who reported to the Terminal Superintendent. Each Terminal also had porters, information desk staff and nursery staff for the children's nursery.

As you will remember from earlier chapters, I started work in the North Terminal with BOAC in 1958. At this time, Terminal 2 in the Central Area had been open since 1955. BEA had transferred its operations from Northolt to this Terminal. The Terminal was named "Europa" because it served Europe, and the south-west end of the building was the domestic

Terminal and called "Britannic." This domestic Terminal was used almost exclusively by BEA, who then had a monopoly on domestic flights.

Terminal 3 came into operation in 1961 when BOAC transferred its services from the North Terminal. The other long-haul airlines followed in 1962 and the North Terminal closed. Terminal 3 was labelled "Oceanic." In those days both Arrivals and Departures were contained within what is now the Departures Building.

Terminal 1 came into operation in 1969 when BEA transferred both its international and domestic services to the new Terminal, which now took on the name "Britannic," leaving all of Terminal 2 as "Europa." These Terminal names have now gone and Terminals are just referred to by their number. However, the original names live on in each Terminal's radio call sign, e.g. all Terminal 1 calls are prefixed 'B' (Bravo), Terminal 2 'E' (Echo) and Terminal 3 'O' (Oscar). When Terminal 4 was opened in 1986 this system could not be continued and Terminal 4 was allocated 'K' (Kilo), one of the few letters in the alphabet not already in use by BAA as a call sign.

One aspect of Passenger Terminals which we now take so much for granted is the profusion of television screens giving flight information. In the early days information about aircraft arrivals and departures was given on wooden boards placed by hand. Then followed the SOLARI flap boards which could be controlled from a central location but, being mechanical, they could still fail. The arrival of the VDU has revolutionised airport communications.

As a rule, passengers in the early 1970s either walked from the Terminal across the Apron to the aircraft or were taken there in a bus. Air jetties were in their infancy. Terminal 3 initially installed some jetties (British-made) which were very complicated in operation, very heavy and prone to breaking down in such a position as to obstruct the Apron and prevent its use by aircraft. These particular jetties were soon abandoned in favour of lighter foreign-made jetties which are now in use in all terminals.

One thing that has changed very noticeably since my early days with the BAA at Heathrow is the change from an ample availability of porters to the present abundance of self-help trolleys which, it is believed, passengers prefer. BAA at Heathrow no longer employs porters but help is always made available free to those who, for reason of disability, age or accompanying infants, cannot cope unaided with their baggage. Skycaps are also available on payment to anyone who requires them and to provide a porterage service to VIPs. The collection and redistribution of trolleys has become a major and labour-intensive operation but Heathrow continues to provide trolleys free in all Terminals and car parks.

My arrival at Heathrow (BAA) in 1970 also coincided with the advent of the first serious measures introduced at airports to counter the threat to aviation posed by international terrorism.

Passengers passing through Heathrow today will be familiar with search procedures, and consent willingly to a stranger searching their baggage and their bodies for concealed weapons or explosives. In the early days, the only search that could take place was one carried out on departure by HM Customs. All passengers used to pass through Customs on arrival and departure.

The fence around Heathrow used to be a ranch-type fence through which people and animals could climb with the greatest of ease and some staff who cycled to work at the airport used to take a short cut across the airfield. I have personally encountered pigs and horses loose on the airfield.

Aviation terrorism is not new – the first hijacking having been reported in 1930. Thereafter, there were minor incidents until the late 1960s, when there was a marked increase in hijackings, usually involving Cuba. Added to this was the growing anti-Israel terrorism which obviously threatened the Israeli airline, EL AL, which operates regularly from Heathrow. I witnessed the arrival at Heathrow of the EL AL 707 hijacked in the Leila Khaled incident.

Nothing I can think of has had such an effect on airport construction and operation as terrorism. Airport Terminals now have to be designed to meet stringent government security requirements. This was possible with Terminal 4 and will be with Terminal 5. The older Terminals 1, 2 and 3 have had to be adapted at considerable cost to meet these requirements.

The object of airport security is to provide a 'sterile area' in all airside areas (those areas departing passengers enter after passing through Immigration and Security checks). This is achieved by screening all passengers, all staff (including the company Chairman and the Airport Director), and all vehicles and goods (including catering supplies for loading onto aircraft). In this way, aircraft always remain in the sterile area and are protected from anything hazardous being taken on board. All this screening and searching is highly labour-intensive and in any Terminal far more staff are employed on security duties than on operating the Terminal. Whatever cost-saving initiatives are introduced, security is never allowed to be reduced.

To sum up the change in security since working at Heathrow: I used to be able to walk through to airside unchallenged. If challenged by Immigration, I just said "staff" and was waved through. Now, even as the manager in charge at the time of the airport I would be required to wear my

ID pass at all times. If I wished to go to airside, my ID photograph would be checked to ensure it was mine and the card itself would then be entered into a machine to ensure it was still valid. Then I and the vehicle, if I was in one, would be subjected to a search.

Heathrow not only has its own inspection procedures to ensure that security standards are maintained, but all UK airports are inspected regularly by Security Inspectors of The Department of Transport who have the authority to stop any airport operating if not satisfied with the standards. It is a serious cause for concern that all foreign governments do not enforce comparable standards at airports under their control.

Commercial activity has increased enormously since the British Airports Authority took over Heathrow from the Ministry and particularly so since the Authority was privatised in 1987; the Authority became BAA plc and Heathrow's management Heathrow Airport Ltd (HAL).

In Ministry days, the greater part of an airport's revenue came from landing fees charged to airlines. Commercial activities were limited to Duty Free sales, catering outlets and newsagents and tobacconists.

There used to be a news cinema in the Queen's Building. It was located in the premises now occupied by the Heathrow Airport Ltd (HAL) Medical Centre. The remains of the old cinema entrance ticket kiosk can still be seen if you enter the Queen's Building by its main entrance. The cinema programme was repeated every hour and so was invaluable for entertaining delayed passengers.

Having said there was only limited commercial activity in the early days, there was no lack of entrepreneurial talent amongst the staff! Terminal 1 and the Ground Operations Unit, for example, could always be relied upon for a supply of fresh vegetables. At one time staff in the Ground Operations

Unit also ran a limousine service with elderly Austin Princess cars. I am told that one of the drivers had to ask for a push at a rather critical moment whilst carrying a funeral party. Almost anything you might require could be obtained through staff. If the person you asked first did not know where to find your requirement, he always knew someone who did! One of our shift-working staff appeared over a long period to have a very poor work attendance on particular day shifts. It was later discovered that this gentleman had a market stall in Hounslow – Heathrow released him to concentrate on his stall!

Although not strictly commercial from an airport revenue point of view, the airfield produced the most magnificent mushrooms. They were certainly the largest I have ever seen and very prolific. It was interesting to see how certain areas of the airfield received exceptional attention from the Operations staff during their early morning surface inspections. There were no complains from ATC, who always had a share of the pickings. Unfortunately, this source of mushrooms has largely disappeared because the airport grass areas have been treated with an insecticide to discourage the birds, which fed on the insects, from visiting the airfield and posing a threat to aircraft. The mushrooms obviously did not appreciate the insecticide!

Now a word about the Motor Transport section, already mentioned in connection with snow clearance. This was a fascinating unit which operated and maintained a great variety of vehicles, some of them relics from The Ministry and almost 'classics' in their own right. The most important vehicles were obviously the Fire Service vehicles. BAA at Heathrow used to operate a combined Fire and Ambulance service. In addition to the special foam-producing fire tenders required for airports, the fire station housed the ambulances and a specially-designed water rescue vehicle in case of an aircraft crashing into one of the many reservoirs around the airport or, worse, into the sewage works. This consisted of an ambulance converted to carry inflatable boats, outboard motors, etc.

To return to the fire appliances – they were of great importance on two counts. Firstly and obviously, they were there to save life, but secondly, their presence was a legal requirement for the operation of aircraft at the airport. Depending on the size of aircraft using an airport, the government requires a specified amount of extinguishing media to be available on appliances and also specifies a time within which the appliances must reach an accident. Heathrow easily meets these requirements but, in the unlikely event of extinguishing media being used up in a serious incident, flying would have to cease until the correct quantities were available.

Apart from the fire vehicles and ambulances, the Motor Transport section (MT) had a huge variety of vehicles with nothing in common except that they were all painted yellow. These vehicles were all purpose-built for such functions as snow clearing, runway sweeping, tunnel cleaning, light cleaning, drain clearing, runway painting, aircraft recovery and salvage, aircraft marshalling, airfield maintenance, mobile lighting and mobile emergency control posts. There were also buses and cars ranging from the basic to those suitable for transporting VIPs.

The MT section was – and is – staffed on a 24-hour basis and drivers allocated to duties as required. One driver is always kept available to drive the medical emergency vehicle to the scene of an accident. This is a large truck carrying all sorts of equipment needed at the scene of an accident such as stretchers, blankets etc., and also brings to the site inflatable tents complete with their own lighting. These tents can be erected very rapidly by

MT staff near the accident and are initially used for 'Triage' (the sorting of injured persons into categories according to the severity of their injuries).

On the lighter side, someone in Head Office decided that Heathrow should have a better vehicle for rescuing people from water or sewage lagoons and designed and had built the 'Tortoise.' This consisted of a large flat platform mounted on four enormous tyres which were not only to provide the buoyancy to enable the platform to float, but the tyres were equipped with fins so that they could also provide the propulsion, rather in the manner of a paddle steamer.

The Tortoise was duly delivered to Heathrow and taken for trials in the Perry Oaks sewage works. I did not personally witness the trials but I was told that, on entry to the sewage, the rear wheels spun, with unhappy consequences for the dignitaries viewing their new toy. In the event, the fins on the tyres became clogged with sewage and progress became slower and slower. The Tortoise was disposed of and Heathrow now has a Hover-craft which works well.

Another peculiar vehicle that appeared at Heathrow was a bomb disposal vehicle. This consisted of a specially-built trailer on which was mounted a cylinder made of heavy steel. The cylinder was mounted vertically with an open end facing skywards. Adjacent to the cylinder was a hoist with which to lift suspicious objects into the cylinder. The theory was that if any device *did* explode in transit, the blast would be directed upwards, thereby minimising the risk to persons and property. The trailer was to be towed by an armour-plated Land Rover which would take the suspicious object to a bomb disposal building in a grass area west of Terminal 3. This building had been built to the specifications supplied by the Metropolitan Police. However, the bomb vehicle was seldom used, for two reasons: later thinking on the subject suggested it unwise to move a suspicious object until cleared by the police, and it had never been established who was going to risk his life hoisting the article into the trailer. The trailer was dismantled and the bomb disposal building is now in use by engineers as a store. Since those days, procedures for dealing with the suspicious objects have advanced enormously and Heathrow Security staff now act as consultants to other transport undertakings in how best to do so.

The MT section also makes an invaluable contribution to keeping the airport operating apart from the snow-clearing activities. One such occasion is when a pilot, in spite of the wide taxiways and runways provided, elects to drive his aeroplane onto the grass, where it sinks. MT has a vehicle ready loaded with all the equipment needed to dig it out and, if necessary, airbags are used to lift the aircraft. Aircraft getting stuck in the soft ground are fairly infrequent but such an event, when it occurs, can be very disrupting to aircraft movements around the airfield and may obstruct a runway.

If Heathrow was said to have an 'Achilles heel,' it would be the main tunnel through which all traffic into and out of the Central Area has to pass. A breakdown in the inbound bore of this tunnel immediately and seriously impedes traffic bound for Terminals 1, 2 and 3 and can cause traffic jams back to the M4. A worse situation for the airport is a breakdown in the outbound tunnel which can quickly bring traffic in the Central Area to a log-jam, which does not rapidly disappear even when the tunnel clears.

It is a credit to the MT staff that their response is swift and the obstruction normally removed before the situation becomes serious. Sometimes the problem is not so readily resolved as, for example, when a bus shed its back axle completely in the tunnel, or when a car transporter, too tall for the tunnel, became firmly wedged between the floor and roof.

One of the most noteworthy occurrences in the 1970s at Heathrow was the arrival and entry into passenger service of Concorde. It first landed at Heathrow on the 13th September 1970, but supersonic passenger services were not started until the 21st January 1976. My wife and I watched this first departure from the top of the Heathrow Control Tower, where we were able to see, on television, the simultaneous departure of the Air France Concorde from Paris.

I am a great supporter of Concorde and have been lucky enough to fly in her twice – London–New York and London–Paris. On another occasion, I took a group of Air Training Corps cadets to visit the British Airways Engineering Base at Heathrow. Whilst they were sitting in a Concorde in the hangar, the engineers said they needed to move it. The aircraft, with the cadets on board, was pushed back out of the hangar and then towed some distance to a remote parking area. The cadets can now truthfully claim that they have travelled in both directions by Concorde!

From a Terminal management point of view the arrival of Concorde caused little difficulty. Terminal 3 was the first to handle this aircraft and dedicated one corner of the departure concourse entirely to Concorde passengers. When British Airways transferred the operations to Terminal 4, check-in area, aircraft stand and special lounge for Concorde had already been provided.

On the Operations side noise was and will always be the major problem. Having said that I think most people who complain about Concorde noise still have a sneaking admiration for this beautiful craft. In the early days of Concorde operating at Heathrow I received a call from a lady claiming that her Ming vase had been shaken off its stand by Concorde and thought Heathrow should pay for it! Another lady who said she was pregnant complained that Concorde caused her unborn child to jump.

Because of its high speed on take-off and landing, Concorde is particularly vulnerable to any debris on the runway, as has been highlighted by the investigation into the recent Air France disaster. To prevent such happenings the Manoeuvring Area Safety Unit carries out regular inspections of all runways.

Before leaving 1970s Heathrow, a few words on the subjects of uniforms, drinking on duty and tipping. Since the early days, substantial changes have been achieved by management in all three of these facets of airport life. Action taken by management on the last two I heartily endorse, but I was never entirely happy with the company uniform policy. This is probably because I am old fashioned and conservative (small 'c'!)

When the BAA took over the airport from the Ministry, the uniform was a traditional military-style black uniform (the style used for flight crew) with silver braid to denote rank. This uniform was smart and the only alteration made by the BAA was to replace the Ministry badge on the cap with the 'Parallel Runway' motif, which was the BAA logo of the time.

The Ministry black uniform was then replaced with a brown uniform with single-breasted jackets. Worn with this brown uniform were a brown shirt and orange tie! Rank markings were in gold and, as an Airport Duty Manager (the highest uniformed rank) my sleeves were adorned with four gold rings and three stars. This was a uniform it was not easy to take a pride in and used to invite rude comments from airline staff about the Brown Army.

The passing of the brown uniform was not mourned by many and was replaced by a much less formal blazer and flannels with almost indistinguishable rank markings. This uniform has been changed again (since I retired) to a green one which you may have noticed in the BBC programme "AIRPORT". This seems to be popular but, if I ever put on another uniform, I would choose a Royal Navy or early BOAC type.

Drinking on duty was not uncommon, and at lunchtime airport bars could be seen to be well-fraternised by airport staff distinguishable by their uniforms. Even staff employed on marshalling duties were permitted to drink. Although I never encountered any very serious drink problems amongst my staff, I was very pleased when management brought in a total ban on alcohol consumption on duty. This ban applied equally to all levels of staff, so was seen to be fair, if not initially popular.

Tipping, and any soliciting or acceptance of gratuities by HAL staff has also been forbidden. There is no doubt that there was a great deal of money to be made in tips, particularly from wealthy Middle Eastern gentlemen! For passengers, tipping was always an uncomfortable business – whether to tip, who to tip and how much. For staff it led to unfairness as some jobs, such as portering or looking after VIPs, gave excellent opportunities to enhance one's income, whilst others doing equally valuable work had no such chances.

At Rome airport, the business of gratuities was so out of hand that at Christmas, airlines had to budget for gifts for all levels of Airport Authority staff. I am sure this has now changed!

CHAPTER FIVE

HEATHROW AIRPORT LIMITED: OPERATIONAL UNITS

After much delay we are now going to look at Heathrow Airport as it was in 1993. That was the year I retired, so if things have changed since, I would not necessarily be aware of them. Heathrow has always been in a state of change, so please bear in mind that the period during which I was personally involved with Heathrow was between 1958 and 1993. Anything I have written about within this period, I believe to be true.

In 1978 the Airport Director decided he needed someone to represent him outside office hours and to take responsibility for the overall safe and efficient operation of the airport on a 24-hour basis. The post of Senior Airport Duty Officer was created to perform this task, reporting directly to the Airport Director. A team of six was to be formed to carry out this task on a shift basis and I was fortunate to be one of the first six. I was even more fortunate in that I was able to stay in this superb job until 1993, with a short interval as Security Manager. The job title was later changed to Airport Duty Manager (ADM) but the radio callsign 'SADO' still reflects the original title. (It has no connections with any strange tendencies ADMs may have had.)

The job content is probably the most interesting available to anyone employed at an airport. There are no facets of airport life or operations with which the ADM does not get involved in some way. Also, it is a job with responsibility and the authority to perform it without reference to anyone higher.

I am writing of Heathrow as seen from the point of view of an Airport Duty Manager, whom I shall hereafter refer to as the ADM for brevity. Much has already been written about Heathrow in terms of passenger throughput, cups of tea sold, aircraft operations, cargo carried etc. Heathrow leads the field in all these things, but I will leave statistics and figures to those who are good at them.

The ADM was based in an office in the Heathrow Airport Ltd Headquarters building called D'Albiac House, but spent the majority of his time around the airport. He was constantly available on radio, whether on foot or in the ADM car which was provided with all necessary radio frequencies and a portable telephone. I must emphasise that I am writing of the ADM as 'he' for convenience and not from any prejudice against lady ADMs; I had some excellent lady ADM colleagues.

If I am to talk about Heathrow as seen by one ADM, I shall first have to explain briefly who does what. I must first apologise to my many ex-colleagues who do essential administrative jobs, working normal hours. My work as an ADM was almost entirely with those working in the front line on a shift basis, so I shall confine myself to the areas I understand. I shall now take each operational section and describe briefly its function.

The Airport Fire Service

Of all the HAL operational units the airport fire service is absolutely essential if any passenger carrying flights are to operate from Heathrow. Each airport in the UK is required by the CAA to provide a level of fire cover. This is described as a Fire Category and is dependent on the size of aircraft using the airport. It stipulates for each category the minimum availability of extinguishing media on wheels. Heathrow naturally has the highest fire category and in reality always exceeds the minimum. The Airport Licence under which Heathrow operates is dependent on satisfying the CAA that all the requirements are met.

Should the fire service be in action at an incident with some appliances employed it can happen that the remaining appliances are insufficient to meet the full fire category. In this case it is the responsibility of the Operations Duty Manager to advise ATC of the reduction in Category and which aircraft can still be accepted.

Heathrow has two fire stations. The main fire station used to be north of Runway 27R/09L and the subsidiary station in the Central Area at the end of one of Terminal 2's piers. Having the main station north of the runway had the disadvantage that in an emergency the fire appliances had to cross the runway which could in turn cause a delay. The main station is now located in the Central Area to the West of Terminal 3, which gives unimpeded access to both runways.

Chapter Eight of this book deals with how the fire service operates in emergencies but I must state here that Heathrow Fire Service has an excellent and well-deserved reputation and shares its skills by training staff of other airports. Because of its special skills and equipment the fire service is at times called upon to assist at non-aviation emergencies. An example of this was when Heathrow equipment was requested and sent to the Clapham rail disaster. When necessary the Heathrow Fire Service also will respond to incidents within a mile and a half of the airport boundary.

In my duties as Operations Duty Manager and Airport Duty Manager I had much involvement with the fire service and was personally involved with the official enquiry into the crash on Runway 05 of the BOAC B.707 G-ARWE (8th April 1968), and with the Trident "Papa India" which crashed in Staines (18th June 1972).

Passenger Terminals

There are at present four passenger Terminals, three in the Central Area and one on the south-east corner of the airport. In charge of each, except during the night hours, is a Terminal Duty Manager. He is, in turn, assisted by Terminal Duty Officers, Security Duty Officers and Terminal Engineering staff, each responsible to him (the TDM) for the staff and responsibilities allocated to them. These would include those on the Information Desk, all the security guards and the Passenger Service staff.

Each Terminal has a Control Centre which is manned at all times and from which all terminal activities can be co-ordinated. All fire alarms, security alarms and lift alarms within the Terminal and adjacent car parks are monitored from this Control Centre and any necessary action taken immediately. The Terminal Control Centre can communicate by public address systems with any part of the Terminal and by radio with any supervisory duty staff, including the TDM and, if necessary, the ADM. As explained earlier, the radio call sign of Terminals 1, 2, 3 and 4 are Bravo, Echo, Oscar and Kilo respectively. If, for example, the TDM in Terminal 3 wished to call the Airport Duty Manager, the call would start thus "SADO, this is Oscar One."

Each Terminal Control Centre also has direct line telephone links with the Heathrow Airport Operations Centre.

Each Terminal operates as a separate unit but is closely involved with the other three because of transfer passengers landing in one terminal and travelling out from another. Heathrow now has a special terminal in the Central Area devoted entirely to transfer passengers

The Heathrow Operations Centre

The Heathrow Operations Centre (HOC) is the communications nerve centre of the airport. Historically the centre is an amalgam of three units which used to operated separately – The Management Duty Room, Apron Control and The Security Communications Centre. (When I joined the BAA at Heathrow the airport nerve centre was the Management Duty Room situated on the roof of Terminal 2. It then moved to D'Albiac House and became the HOC. It is now called the Star Centre and includes the Engineering Control Centre.)

The HOC is manned continuously and its staff undertake several vital functions. The most important of these is the co-ordination of activities on the airport during an emergency whether it be an aircraft accident, building fire or terrorist threat. The HOC staff are trained in the appropriate action to be taken in any emergency, they know who to advise and what needs to be recorded. They also provide a vital service to the ADM who might be at some remote part of the airport when the emergency starts. They keep him advised by radio and issue instructions on his behalf.

HOC has direct telephone lines to such agencies as Air Traffic Control, Airport Police, Terminal Control Centres etc. and, of course, radio communications with all sections. After an emergency is over the log of events kept by HOC is often used in subsequent investigations.

HOC maintains a constant liaison with ATC and allocates parking stands for incoming aircraft. This sounds simple but, with an airport operating near to its capacity, there is little room for flexibility. The stand allocated must be of a size to accommodate the particular aircraft type, be convenient for the airline and have serviceable jetties (passenger walkways).

If aircraft operated close to their schedule times all this allocation could be pre-planned but, as this ideal is rarely achieved, it takes very experienced staff to obtain the optimum utilisation from the available stands and, at the same time, give a good service to the airlines.

All information boards and television displays for the public are computer-operated. It is the responsibility of HOC to supervise this operation, ensure information displayed is correct and take remedial action when anything is amiss. HOC also collects a mass of data on aircraft operations on behalf of the Finance Department to enable them to assess parking and landing charges.

One of the most varied and, at times, taxing task for HOC is being the main point of contact for any airlines, Control Authorities or members of the public. If, for example, there is an aircraft accident anywhere in the world, HOC receives masses of calls from worried friends/relatives. If, in the rare event of an aircraft from Heathrow being involved, HOC is immediately swamped with calls from the Press.

In the 'good old days,' airlines used to have staff available at night to provide flight information on their flights. Now the best a caller will get from an airline at night is a recording, which is obviously only accurate at the time it was made. People are often not satisfied with this and call Heathrow Airport. Such calls end up with HOC.

In addition to calls connected with aviation, HOC receives calls for information on bus and train services, shipping, welfare services and even calls from people contemplating suicide. Some are not as serious: on one night a man rang HOC to say he had to reach some remote part of China urgently. HOC staff did a lot of research to find the quickest way of getting this man to his destination. On calling him back with the results of their efforts, they were rewarded with: "Thanks – you have helped me win a bet at this party!"

HOC have the radio call sign 'Control.'

Engineering Control Centre

In the same way as the Heathrow Operations Centre is the hub of all communications on operational matters, the Engineering Control Centre monitors all the technical aspects of the airport. In this Centre will be found the Airport Duty Engineering Manager (formerly called the Control Engineer), a very experienced engineer who needs to be knowledgeable on civil, electrical and mechanical engineering.

Heathrow is a city in its own right with all the attendant problems of maintaining in perfect condition such vital services as power supplies, water supplies, drains and sewage, buildings, car parks and roads. In other respects it differs from an ordinary city in that it depends for its operation on an immense and varied amount of electronic and mechanical equipment.

A few examples of Heathrow's specialised equipment should suffice to make the point. Well over 50 million passengers pass through the airport every year. Equipment has to be provided in all Terminals to X-ray the baggage of the passengers, conveyors to carry their baggage from check-in to the baggage sorting area where other machines read the baggage labels and allocate them to correct flights. The airport stores and distributes, via a hydrant system, enormous quantities of aviation fuel. All the aircraft stands are equipped with hydrants, so there is no need for the traditional fuel bowser.

Heathrow also differs from an ordinary city in that its continued use by aircraft is dependent on very strict standards being met in terms of airfield lighting, runway and taxiway surface condition and safeguarding (absence of hazardous obstructions in operational areas, including runway approaches).

All operational areas are constantly inspected by Operations staff but any necessary remedial action is usually the responsibility of the Airport Duty Engineering Manager (ADEM). The standards imposed on an airport are particularly stringent in connection with equipment associated with All Weather Operations (CAT 3).

Like the ADM, the ADEM is primarily concerned with the safety of all at Heathrow, whether they be in aircraft, in passenger terminals, car parks or on the airport roads. This encompasses passengers, staff, 'meeters and greeters' and even uninvited guests (vagrants – of whom more later).

The ADM and ADEM need to work closely together as many of their problems overlap. I recall one very difficult Saturday night duty for us both. A contractor, working on an extension to Terminal 1, had been excavating for laying foundations and filling the deep holes so made with concrete. Because it was Saturday, the contractor's staff went home at midday. Later in the day it was found that they had dug through, and filled with concrete, the large-diameter and only sewage pipe from the Central Area of the airport! This required rapid co-operative action from the ADEM and the

ADM. All use of water in the Terminals had to be reduced to an absolute minimum as drain covers were already lifting with the pressure of sewage in some parts of the airport. All catering outlets had to stop washing up and obviously the water supply to the public and staff toilets had to be turned off. One toilet was left open in each Terminal for those *in extremis*!

Engineers estimated that it would be a matter of days before the pipe could be restored to use and, in the meantime, plans were made to divert the sewage via flexible hoses around the blocked pipe. This involved taking the pipe across a main airport road. The flexible pipe was too large for a ramp to be used to enable vehicles to cross it so it had to be raised above the road. Huge pumps were obtained and engineers worked through the night to effect the temporary sewage system. Whilst this temporary system was being established, the road traffic flow in the area had to be reversed. This was only possible during the night but would have been catastrophic after 06.00 when traffic inbound to the Central Area starts to build up.

At about 05.30, the engineers announced that all was finished and I went to the site to restore the road system to normal. The pumps were started up and, instead of the sewage flowing smoothly out of the Central Area, the pipe nearest the pumps started to swell alarmingly! Needless to say, I retired rapidly to my car before the pipe burst. The pumps were turned off before disaster struck. To my great relief, at 06.00 all was well; roads were returned to normal and our passengers could, once again, relieve themselves!

Airfield Safety

The title is relatively new for the department that used to be called Operations. The title of Operations is now applied to Terminals, car parks, roads etc. and not to those sections previously considered Operations etc., the Motor Transport Section, the Fire Service (which I have already mentioned), the Manoeuvring Area Safety Unit and the Apron Safety Unit.

Because the departmental title change is fairly new, this does result in some anomalies. For example, the manager in charge of the Airfield Safety Sections on a 24-hour basis is still the Operations Duty Manager (formerly called the Duty Operations Officer). The radio call sign of the Manoeuvring Area Safety Unit (MASU) is still 'Ground Ops.' Confused? Don't worry – Heathrow staff adapt well to change, having had plenty of practice!

The Manoeuvring Area Safety Unit (formerly Ground Operations) was started in 1968 with eight staff selected from the Marshalling section for special training in performing certain airfield inspection duties previously carried out by ATC staff. They were initially trained by ATC and still work in very close co-operation with them. As the title implies, the Manoeuvring Area Safety Unit is responsible for the safety of the runways, runway approaches, taxiways and all the grass areas surrounding them. This is achieved by constant vigilance, routine inspections of all runways and taxiways, checking the state of the surface and the thousands of light fittings therein. Regular checks are also made on the approach lights for each runway and on the Visual Approach Aids (Precision Approach Path Indicators).

A better publicised part of the MASU task is that of keeping the airfield clear of birds. This is achieved by discouraging birds from settling on the ground at Heathrow by destroying insects upon which they might feed, keeping the grass at a height recommended by bird experts, and by co-operating with Local Authorities over the siting of refuse dumps near the airport, as these invariably attract birds. If the birds do arrive on the airport, they are dispersed by the use of pyrotechnics or by broadcasting recordings of bird distress calls. Regular bird patrols are carried out by MASU and always before the first of the early-morning flight arrivals.

Another of MASU's tasks – a most important one – is the supervision of all engineering works being carried out on the airfield. All such work is carried out under strict safety conditions applied to each job by the Operations Duty Manager. The engineering contractor is given a Works Permit by the ODM giving him these safety conditions. When any work is in progress, MASU will ensure a permit exists and the conditions are being complied with. Apart from Christmas Day, there is always engineering work in progress – either in connection with new developments or in maintaining the existing surface in good order.

During snow conditions, MASU is responsible for reporting on the airfield state to ATC and to the ODM, who issues a 'Snowtam' and MOTNE messages which advise other airports of Heathrow's condition. The information includes, for each runway, the nature and depth of any deposit, the coefficient of friction and any snow banks adjacent to runways or taxiways. (Snowtams are Notams relating to snow and are issued when there is significant change in information. MOTNEs are sent every half hour over the European Met. Office telecommunications network)

Because of the huge expanse of concrete, all runways and taxiways are divided into blocks which are individually numbered. Between each block is a row of red lights set into the surface, which may be switched on by ATC to isolate a block. Along the centre of all taxiways are green lights which are switched on, as necessary, by ATC to delineate a safe route from any part of the airfield to another. Thus, it is simple to direct aircraft on the surface and to identify any area with ease. This becomes essential during emergencies.

That, briefly, is the area of responsibility of MASU staff and is one of the most interesting jobs, if you like close contact with aeroplanes and, at times, with objects dropped from them! An amazing collection exists of items collected by MASU on taxiways and runways which have fallen from aircraft. On one occasion, a Boeing 747 was departing from Runway 28R when it shed a main wheel tyre while at speed down the runway. The tyre sped into a car park where it seriously damaged a new Ford Convertible, having first broken through a substantial steel fence. The cause was a broken wheel, part of which was found on the runway.

The Apron Safety Unit (ASU) has similar responsibilities to those of MASU but their area of responsibility is the Apron areas. These comprise some 175 aircraft parking stands. Each stand has to be inspected for safety with respect to its surface, lighting, jetties, parking guidance systems and for obstructions in the form of equipment or refuse incorrectly left on the stands by airline staff.

The Apron Safety Unit was originally called the Marshalling Section and this still describes part of their function. Generally, aircraft operating at Heathrow are directed by ATC between the runways and stands by the use of green taxiway lights or by reference to block numbers. On arrival at the stands, Visual Guidance Systems are provided to enable the pilot to position his aircraft on the stand centreline and to stop it at the right spot and so be aligned with the jetty.

Not infrequently, aircraft arrive at Heathrow whose crews are unfamiliar with the airport, and such aircraft are provided with a full 'Leader' ("Follow Me") service by ASU.

Whenever there is work going on on the airfield, contractors' vehicles need to travel to and from the works site without endangering themselves or aircraft. To achieve this safely, an escort is provided by the ASU vehicles which are always in radio contact with ATC.

During snow conditions, the ASU is responsible for snow clearance on all aircraft parking stands and for ensuring that no lights used for aircraft guidance are obscured.

However, the most important function for the ASU occurs during aircraft emergencies when they are responsible for leading fire appliances and ambulances to the scene and subsequently for assembling airline support vehicles such as coaches and loading vehicles and taking them to the scene of the incident. This will be dealt with in a later chapter on 'Aircraft Emergencies.'

Ground Security

The Ground Security Unit operates on a shift basis under the direction of the Ground Security Duty Manager, and is responsible for scrutinising all persons and vehicles attempting to gain access to Airside areas (except those passing through passenger terminals). All persons and vehicles are subject to search, and the ID cards are all checked to ensure that the photograph thereon is that of the presenter and the card itself is checked by card reader for validity.

Inevitably, there are vehicles needing access to airside areas such as engineering contractors' vehicles, private ambulances and VIP vehicles which arrive at Heathrow without the correct documentation. None of these is given access until approval has been given by the ADM. The delay can, at times, annoy the VIP so inconvenienced, but it is essential that this rigid control is maintained. The cause of the incorrect documentation is, in any case, a failure of the VIP's office or embassy to comply with the correct procedures.

The Ground Security Unit also carries out constant patrols of all airside areas and regular checks of perimeter fencing. All vehicles on airside are required to display a special identification so that any vehicle that should not be there is readily noticed. All staff are taught to be vigilant about such things, but it is a particular responsibility of the Ground Security Unit.

Another task undertaken by the Ground Security Unit is the searching of aircraft on behalf of airlines. The Unit has staff expert in this operation.

Ground Transportation

However efficient an airport is in terms of aircraft handling and passenger processing, this is of little use if getting to and from the airport, and parking when you get there, proves difficult. Heathrow is already well served by motorway links, buses, the Underground and will shortly be operating its own high-speed rail link.

At the airport, car parks are provided to suit all customers. Those in the ones adjacent to the passenger Terminals are the most expensive and are intended for short-term parking. Further from the terminals are the Business Parks which provide free transport to the appropriate terminal within a guaranteed time – if the time is exceeded, you can claim a refund. For those leaving their cars for a longer period, there is the Long Term car park, which offers the cheapest rates.

Numerous coach operators route through Heathrow using the Central Area coach station. Heathrow is such a good coach centre that we once discovered that a shipping company was briefing passengers to assemble in

Terminal 1 before boarding the shipping company's coach to Southampton! The BAA was unknowingly providing the shipping company with a London terminal.

To ensure all runs smoothly in all areas of roads, trains, buses, car parks etc., Heathrow Airport Ltd has a Ground Transportation Unit and, at any time of the day or night, there is a Ground Transportation Duty Officer to sort out any problems.

Occasionally the problems encountered by the Duty Officers do not have a simple solution and lead them to calling for police assistance. Examples are serious road accidents, the discovery of thieves or vandals in car parks or drunks and vagrants causing problems in car parks.

Much of the Duty Officer's time is spent in helping customers with their questions or problems. At 02.00 one morning, a Duty Officer was on his rounds in the coach station when he saw a woman lying on the pavement. He naturally asked if she needed help and she replied: "Yes. Can you tell me what time the tide comes in?" For once, a ready answer was not forthcoming!

On another night, the Duty Officer was called to the Eastern Perimeter Road where a policeman was reported to have been attacked by a driver. His investigation revealed that the driver, who was very drunk, had earlier crashed his car damaging it in such a way that he could only engage reverse gear. He had therefore decided to drive home backwards. When he was stopped by a police car, he assaulted the policeman. He was a guest of the police that night!

Special Facilities

Heathrow Airport provides VIP lounges which it staffs and operates on behalf of the Foreign and Commonwealth Office. The VIP suites are within, or close to, the passenger terminals, apart from the Royal Suite, which is deliberately sited well away from public areas.

With the exception of the Terminal 3 suite – the Hillingdon suite – all the suites are relatively new. Originally the Royal Suite was on North Side near the Met. Office. Terminal 1 had the de Havilland Suite, The Queen's Building had the Kingsford-Smith Suite, Terminal 2 had the Brabazon Suite and Terminal 3 had the Alcock & Brown Suite (now renamed the Hillingdon). Terminals 1 and 2 are now served by one new suite, the Hounslow Suite and Terminal 4 by the Spelthorne Suite. It may have been politically expedient, but I was sorry to see the disappearance from suite names of famous aviation pioneers.

However, all connection with the past is not lost – the statue of Alcock and Brown still stands proudly near the Control Tower, a site to which it was moved from its original position adjacent to the North Terminal.

Heathrow Airport staff, known as Special Facilities Officers, look after VIPs in the suites and escort them to and from their aircraft, arrange their check-in, baggage delivery, Customs clearance etc.

The airport does not decide who should be given VIP status by the government and bookings for the various suites are made by government offices or foreign embassies.

One of the difficult problems associated with looking after VIPs is the size of the retinue travelling with them – some foreign dignitaries seem to travel with their entire household staff and are surrounded, on arrival or departure, by large numbers of embassy staff. Cars from the respective embassy are led out to the aircraft to collect or deliver the VIP – on one occasion, there were 27 limousines to meet 26 passengers!

VIPs are, in the main, senior ministers of foreign and commonwealth nations, senior diplomats, members of ruling families, very senior Service officers, UN officials and important guests of HM Government.

Another problem Special Facilities Officers (SFO) encounter are people who think they are entitled to the VIP suite but have not been booked into one. This can either be an error by an embassy or the person may not be entitled. In either case, the matter has to be resolved rapidly and diplomatically.

Special Facilities Officers are available from 06.00–23.00 and outside these hours the VIPs are looked after by the Airport Duty Manager. This system works well unless there are simultaneous arrivals in different suites or when the ADM is called away because of an emergency. I was, one morning, looking after a prime minister when advised on the radio of a fire in the Control Tower. I had to abandon the poor man to accompanying the other passengers through normal channels.

In some 15 years as an ADM I met an enormous variety of VIPs, most of whom were gracious and interesting to speak to. Those I did not appreciate were the self-important and arrogant – the type well described as 'self-made men who worship their maker'!

Because of their tendency to attend late functions, members of the British Royal Family often arrive at Heathrow so late that the ADM has to meet them. I was privileged to meet most of them. On one occasion I had met a duchess and taken her to the Royal Suite where we waited for her car to collect her. We waited what seemed an age and the Lady was obviously tired and keen to be home. Eventually a magnificent Rolls Royce arrived and an elderly chauffeur came into the Suite. The Duchess said: "Hello, Bill; was it the traffic that delayed you?" I shall never forget his reply: "No, Ma'am, you were early."

One of my more embarrassing experiences with VIPs was when I met Mr Kenyatta at the Brabazon Suite. As I led him out to his car we came face to face with a large banner saying "Hang Kenyatta" being displayed by a protest group. This could not happen now as all the suites are on the airside, but some of the old suites were on landside.

On another occasion, I had met a princess from the Far East and escorted her to the suite with a number of staff from the embassy. I later had to enter the suite and found the princess seated and everyone else prostrate on the floor. Apparently, one has to remain physically below royalty. As the only one standing I felt a little conspicuous, and retired rapidly.

Terminals can experience serious problems of public order and congestion if, without prior notice to the airport, a well-known "pop star" or Eastern religious leader passes through the Terminal. In either of these cases the Terminal can be swamped with hundreds of fanatical followers who wish to demonstrate their devotion to their 'idol' or guru.

If the airport is given prior warning of any such person travelling, special arrangements are made in co-operation with the police, to enable the followers to show their devotion without disrupting Heathrow.

Public Affairs (formerly called Public Relations)

The Public Affairs Department at Heathrow is not operational, in the sense that its staff are normally not at the airport 24-hours a day but, in the event of an emergency, it rapidly becomes so. When there is a major incident, the presence of Public Affairs staff on the airport is invaluable to the Airport Duty Manager in allowing him to concentrate on the incident whilst the media representatives are attended to by the specialist staff. The Airport Duty Manager is trained in speaking to the media, but in the case of a serious incident, he really has only time to keep Public Affairs staff up-to-date and leave them to brief the press.

I have had personal reason to be grateful to Public Affairs staff on many occasions, but particularly when I was the ADM on the night of the Lockerbie disaster and their speedy arrival at the airport helped me enormously.

Under normal conditions, the Public Affairs Department works normal hours, but one member of staff is always on call at home for dealing with the press queries and reacting to emergencies.

Apart from the tasks already mentioned, Public Affairs is dedicated to the promoting and maintaining of good relations between Heathrow Airport and its passengers, its customer airlines, local residents, Local Authorities and local businesses.

To achieve the above, the airport has an Environment Policy, whose stated objectives are to: reduce disturbance from aircraft operations, improve air and water quality, improve energy efficiency, minimise the use of environmentally sensitive materials, promote recycling and the use of recycled materials and minimise waste and reduce consumption of materials.

Heathrow is of enormous economic benefit to the surrounding area in providing employment and generating business. The airport is also actively involved in local charities, community projects and conservation schemes.

In spite of all Heathrow does, it cannot please everybody. On one Sunday afternoon, I was accosted by a huge West Indian lady who said she wished to make a complaint. I listened politely but, having heard the complaint, could do little to help. She had complained: "There are far too many Indians in this Terminal."

Over a period of time we got frequent complaints from a man living under the approach to runway 27L that pieces of aircraft kept falling off aircraft and breaking the glass of his conservatory. Each time he reported a fall, MASU staff went to the house to recover the items that had fallen, in an endeavour to identify it. It soon became evident that the pieces of metal collected had no connection with aviation. With police assistance, the true origin of these objects was found: children in a nearby scrapyard had rigged a catapult with which they were bombarding this poor man's house!

In spite of the advantages conferred on the local community by Heathrow and the efforts of the Public Affairs Department, there still remains the unavoidable problem of aircraft noise. The responsibility for regulating aircraft noise and night flights belongs to the Department of Transport, but Heathrow is very conscious of the problem and acts to reduce to the minimum (within safety constraints) the effect of aircraft noise on local residents.

The Department of Transport dictates what maximum noise levels may be produced by aircraft and the maxima are lower at night. The Department also limits the number of aircraft operations during the night period (23.00–06.30). All aircraft departing from Heathrow are given departure routes by ATC which are Preferential Noise Routes (PNRs), which will take the aircraft over the least populated areas until it reaches 4000 ft. Strict adherence to the noise limits and the PNRs is mandatory and Heathrow monitors every aircraft movement to ensure compliance. Noise monitoring equipment is placed at strategic points around Heathrow which automatically feeds this information into a computer at Heathrow. Into the Heathrow noise computer is also fed information from the ATC radar so that the track taken by any aircraft and the noise produced by it can be readily established after the event. This not only greatly assists in investigating noise complaints but enables the airport to identify the culprit and, if appropriate, fine a persistent offender.

Arriving aircraft are also required to operate in such a way as to create the minimum noise. This means that they may not descend below 2500 ft until they intercept the ILS Glidepath (approximately eight miles from touchdown), must refrain from descending below the Glidepath and maintain a 'low power/low drag' approach.

The testing of aircraft engines on the ground is also a potential nuisance to local residents and is strictly controlled and monitored by the Operations Duty Manager (ODM) and his staff. He has authority to stop any such running if not done correctly. The ODM also keeps a close watch on all delayed flights to ensure they do not infringe the night noise restrictions. The ODM will, if necessary, prevent any such infringement by getting ATC to refuse departure clearance to the aircraft. The ODM does have the discretion to allow a delayed aircraft to depart within the restricted period in certain rare circumstances where to refuse would cause undue suffering.

In addition to all the above, Heathrow takes other actions to reduce the noise problem. The airport's pricing policy gives great financial benefits to quiet aircraft. The airport operates its main runways in such a way that one is used for departures and one for arriving aircraft. At 15.00 each day this is alternated so that, if you have been under landing aircraft all morning, you will be relieved of them at 15.00 and have a peaceful afternoon.

Heathrow funds and administers a scheme of noise insulation grants to help residents living in areas severely affected by aircraft noise and can provide 100% of the cost of sound-proofing appropriate rooms.

I have taken rather a wide view of Public Affairs, but you cannot isolate any aspect of Heathrow's operation from the Department. Apart from the night of the Lockerbie disaster there were two other noteworthy occasions when I was very grateful for their assistance. One was the night of the first flight returning British hostages from Iraq when the airport was swarming with media personnel and government officials, and the other, the day when Michael Jackson gave a concert at the airport.

Heathrow Medical Centre

Situated on the ground floor of the Queen's Building is the Heathrow Airport Medical Centre which is manned between the hours 06.00–22.00. The Centre offers treatment for all airport users and continuous health monitoring of all Heathrow Airport Ltd employees. The Unit also provides a service to many emergency and stretcher cases which pass through the airport.

One night I was contacted by the duty nurse who had a problem she could not resolve – a private ambulance had delivered a stretcher case festooned with tubes and drips for onward carriage on a certain African airline. The stretcher case had been booked, but when the aircraft arrived they found that the equipment for carrying a stretcher was not on board. The original ambulance had gone, the airline disclaimed responsibility and the London Ambulance Service would not carry a private patient back to a private clinic. We were stuck with a body. I persuaded British Airways to assist on behalf of the original airline, whom they handled, and a private ambulance was obtained to be recharged to the African airline.

All employees of the Medical Centre are part of the first response team sent to any aircraft emergency. The Centre is always alerted when an aircraft is known to be in trouble. A vehicle from MASU comes immediately to the Centre and stands by to take staff to the accident should it happen. There the Centre staff would meet up with the emergency medical vehicle delivered to the site by MT, as explained in a previous chapter.

Each year Heathrow has a full-scale emergency exercise in which a serious aircraft accident is simulated. This is to exercise all sections and organisations who would be involved in a real accident. Volunteer casualties are realistically made up to represent a variety of injuries.

On one such exercise our Principal Nursing Sister was sorting out the fake casualties at the accident site where the light was fairly dim, and asked a volunteer lying on the ground: "What is meant to be wrong with you, young man?"

He replied: "I am supposed to have a broken leg, but at the moment you are standing on my hand!"

As an Airport Duty Manager I always received the greatest co-operation, with a good few cups of coffee, from the Medical Centre staff.

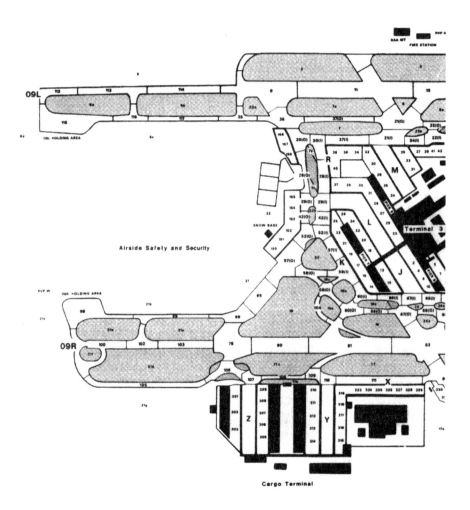

Airside Safety and Security

Cargo Terminal

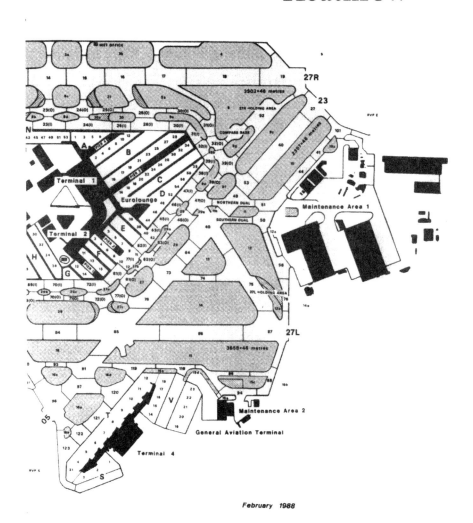

February 1988

CHAPTER SIX

OTHER HEATHROW ORGANISATIONS

In the previous chapter I have outlined what various sections at Heathrow do. Those described were all sections staffed and operated by Heathrow Airport Ltd. In this chapter I will introduce other units not operated by HAL but which make a great contribution to the smooth running of the airport. I have deliberately not covered the operation of the airlines under this chapter as it is a separate subject. This is in no way intended to diminish their importance. Without them Heathrow would not exist and they and their passengers are the airport's very valuable customers.

Heathrow exists to give the airlines a first class and, above all, safe environment in which to operate. There are over 90 passenger airlines operating from Heathrow, each headed variously by a Station Manager, Airport Manager or Airline Representative who together form the Airline Operators Committee which represents the airlines to HAL. On a day-to-day basis the airlines would deal with HAL duty staff and if necessary the ADM on any operational problem.

Without the next two non-HAL organisations, ATC and TELS, this airport could not operate at all.

Air Traffic Control

The Air Traffic Control service at Heathrow is provided by the National Air Traffic Services (NATS) which is a branch of the Civil Aviation Authority

(CAA). The NATS is also responsible for the supervision of all air traffic in the UK-controlled airspace, i.e. airways, terminal control areas and the control zones of most major aerodromes.

All air traffic in the southern half of England comes under the jurisdiction of the London Air Traffic Control Centre (LATCC) which is now situated at West Drayton but was originally on the North Side at Heathrow. An aircraft inbound to Heathrow is under the control of LATCC at West Drayton until told to change radio frequency and contact Heathrow's Approach Control Unit, which was situated in the Heathrow Control Tower below the Visual Control Room (VCR). The VCR is that topmost part of the Control Tower surrounded in glass to enable the ATC staff to have a good view of the approaches to the runways and the runways and taxiways.

In contrast, the Approach Controllers sit in a darkened room in front of a bank of radar screens and instruct pilots to adjust height, speed and direction to achieve a single and properly separated stream of aircraft approaching the runway.

At approximately eight miles from touchdown, Approach Control will hand over an aircraft to the Arrivals Controller in the VCR. For the approach, the aircraft will be established on the ILS and the pilot will receive his landing clearance from the Arrivals Controller, who will also supply him with information on wind strength and direction and any relevant information on the runway state, e.g. water or snow on the surface.

Note. The Heathrow Approach Control Unit has now been transferred to LATCC.

Once clear of the runway, an aircraft comes under the control of the Ground Movements Controller, who will direct it to the appropriate stand. The advice as to which is the correct stand will have been given to ATC by the Heathrow Operations Centre well before the landing. The Ground Movements Controller is in charge of all movement on the airfield and operates on a separate radio frequency. On the GMC radio frequency are all taxying aircraft, all aircraft under tow, HAL works vehicles, Operations vehicles of the MASU and ASU and all Heathrow-based Emergency Vehicles such as the Fire Service, Police, the ADM, ADEM and ODM.

In poor visibility or at night the Ground Movement Controller has at his disposal a special radar, the Aerodrome Surface Movement Indicator (ASMI), which enables him to see all vehicles and aircraft on the airfield and, to assist him in directing aircraft, he has a colleague who is the Lighting Controller. This Controller has before him a large plan of the airfield and, as explained in the previous chapter, can bring up a green route of lights to guide an aircraft from any one part of the airfield to any other.

When an aircraft is ready to depart from Heathrow, it first obtains start-up clearance from ATC and is then cleared to push back from its stand. It also receives its airways clearance which is normally a Standard Instrument Departure (a SID) which will incorporate the required noise abatement procedures (PNRs referred to in the last chapter). It is then given taxi directions by the GMC Controller to take it to the holding point of the departure runway. Near the runway holding point, the GMC Controller tells the aircraft to change radio frequency to that of the Departures Controller. The Departure Controller then sequences the aircraft to achieve the best departure rate. Once the aircraft is airborne it is passed by Heathrow ATC to LATCC.

Heathrow ATC has a wonderful reputation and is respected by pilots of all nationalities for its helpfulness, efficiency and, above all, safety. On a shift basis the link between Heathrow Airport Ltd and ATC is the Operations Duty Manager, whose office is in the Control Tower. Also MASU are in constant radio communication with ATC in the course of their inspection duties.

An aircraft arrival rate of 34 per hour, and departure rate of 37 per hour (these figures by the year 2000 have risen to 42 and 45 respectively) used to represent the peak hours. The peak now extends for the best part of the day, which gives few breaks for MASU to carry out their runway inspections. This is still achieved by the very close co-operation between ATC and MASU.

The excellence of Heathrow's Air Traffic Control and the good communications that exist are in stark contrast with those prevailing at Palam Airport, New Delhi, when a QANTAS Captain and I brought the airport to a halt in 1959. Captain McKnight had landed his QANTAS Boeing 707 and had experienced serious aquaplaning and skidding. Before departing again he said he wished to inspect the runway because it was in the monsoon season and he suspected there was standing water on the runway. A brief check was made with ATC that no inbound aircraft were imminent and he and I went to find a taxi to take us down the runway! We found a taxi on landside and set forth through the police post guarding airside. Although it was dark, the policeman recognised the taxi driver as a wanted man and duly arrested him. The only other vehicle available to us was the large BOAC passenger bus, so we set off again and this time reached the far end of the runway, which was indeed very wet – so wet that the engine of the bus quit. We had no means of communicating to ATC that the runway was blocked by a bus other than to walk back through the torrential rain to the Control Tower. An aircraft tug was then dispatched to retrieve the coach and a very damp Captain rejoined his First Officer who was beginning to worry about his disappearance. Fortunately, the movement rate at Palam did not compare with present-day Heathrow and no serious risk to aviation resulted.

Civil Aviation Authority Telecommunications

CAA Telecommunications (TELS) staff carry out a less glamorous job than their other CAA colleagues in ATC, but one that is equally important and essential to the safety of aircraft. The control of Air Traffic relies entirely upon sophisticated electronic/radio equipment which must be kept in peak condition at all times.

Let us consider the various pieces of TELS equipment involved in the arrival at Heathrow of an inbound aircraft. First, ATC must be able to have voice communication with the aircraft. This means providing the appropriate transmitters and receivers for all the necessary frequencies (air band 115-145 mHz) for each phase of the inbound journey.

Aircraft are routed along airways which aircraft follow by reference to beacons (normally VORs) which are set up and maintained by TELS – in some of the most inaccessible places The entire country is covered by radar which, again, requires TELS to set up radar units in some remote areas. The radar enables ATC to safeguard aircraft by maintaining a safe separation between them on airways and to guide them onto the ILS (another piece of TELS equipment) in such a way that they arrive on the runway at intervals which maintain safe separation and maximum runway utilisation. At points on the ILS are marker beacons which indicate to the pilot his distance from the runway threshold. Finally, the pilot in low visibility will be given the Runway Visual Range from the TELS Transmissometer.

At Heathrow, the man in charge of TELS on a 24-hour basis is the Duty TELS Officer and he and his team keep all the equipment running smoothly. In recent years there has been a proliferation of private radio networks operated by couriers, taxis and car hire companies. These radios tend to wander off their frequency and my dealing with the Duty TELS Officer was usually to ask him to trace the offenders who were causing serious interference to the Airports Management's radio network. This could be very dangerous, particularly when it affected the Fire Service radio. There were occasions where our emergency frequencies were interrupted by cab drivers ordering their breakfast etc.

The reliability of the CAA equipment in this country is excellent and any unserviceabilities short-lived. This is in stark contrast with the state of Navigation Aids in parts of Africa and Asia in the days of BOAC when it was quite a surprise when certain beacons actually worked!

Note: Heathrow has now re-equipped itself with a trunk radio system in order to overcome interference with its management and emergency radio frequencies.

The Airport Police

Heathrow is a city in most respects and, as any city, it needs policing. When the BAA first took over the airport, it had its own police force, the BAA Constabulary, presided over by a Chief Constable. The difference between Heathrow and many cities is that, by and large, the citizens are all friendly towards the police and ready to help them.

In November 1974 the Metropolitan Police formed an airport division to police Heathrow, and the BAA Constabulary was disbanded, with some of the BAA police transferring to the MET. The old BAA police dog-training ground can still be seen between Perry Oaks Sewage Works and Block 115.

The officer in charge of the MET police at Heathrow was initially a Commander, and latterly a Chief Superintendent. On a shift basis, the officer in charge is the Duty Inspector. As an Airport Duty Manager, I had much to do with various levels of the policy hierarchy, but the most valuable relationship was that formed with the Duty Inspectors.

Apart from the routine law enforcement required by any city, Heathrow is special in that it concentrates, in one relatively small area, high-value people and high-value commodities (cargo). High-value people, such as national leaders, diplomats, royalty etc. are always at some risk from 'cranks' and those who do not agree with them. Aircraft and nationals of countries antagonistic to one another are brought into close proximity. With all the conflicts going on at any one time across the world, such meetings at Heathrow are almost inevitable.

The problem of high-value cargo is self-evident, whether it be legitimate or otherwise (drugs). Heathrow police, at one stage, received criticism for the level of theft but this has now ceased. What had not been taken fully into account was how large a port Heathrow is in terms of cargo handled.

Another point in which Heathrow differs from an ordinary city is that it is susceptible to aviation terrorism: it is undoubtedly a prestige target of any terrorists wishing to draw attention to their cause, and this adds a further problem for all airport staff, and especially the police. This is one of the reasons for police officers overtly carrying firearms in certain areas of the airport – probably the first such practice anywhere in the UK.

The police also play a vital role in the event of any emergency, be it a building fire, a road accident, a bomb threat or an aircraft accident. We shall be looking at the role of the police in a later chapter, but suffice it to say that whenever there is an emergency, the ADM and the Duty Inspector confer at the earliest possible opportunity to establish a common approach to the incident.

In an emergency of whatever nature, the HAL staff and police work well together and can each be of great assistance to the other, as both have specialist knowledge and have their own radio communications systems. Terminal staff can also assist police in apprehending criminals.

Our staff in Terminal 3 were watching the Arrivals concourse on closed circuit television and noted a lady pushing a man in a wheelchair. The lady was then seen to drop her purse on the floor, scattering her coins. Another lady bent down to assist, and while she did so her bag was snatched by a third party and concealed in a large shopping bag. This had been a team operation – the wheelchair couple and the bag snatcher. Fortunately our staff were able to lead the police straight to the stolen bag and the police arrested rogues they had long been hoping to catch.

One of the most difficult problems for the airport management and police to resolve is that of vagrants and mentally disturbed people who gravitate to Heathrow, where they can find warmth and sometimes food in the passenger terminals. It is an offence to remain on the airport without good cause and, if asked to leave by a constable or member of the airport management, it is a breach of the airport byelaws not to do so.

HAL staff are very tolerant with vagrants, especially in cold weather, and many of them are such regulars that they are known by name. However, they have to be moved on if they start annoying passengers or begging. If necessary, staff then ask for police assistance in removing them from Heathrow but inevitably they soon turn up again, usually in another

Terminal! There is no real answer to this problem as most of them should be in institutional care, but the government policy seems to be to release them into a community not geared up to cope. There are, of course, some of them who would not settle in 'care' but seem happy to settle at Heathrow!

There is one man who tends to sit in the cafeteria in Terminal 1 and, whilst people around him are enjoying their refreshments, he rolls up his trouser let and picks the scabs on his leg! He hopes they will abandon their food so that he may enjoy it.

There is a little lady who has discovered that the Ladies toilet in the Terminal 3 is an ideal place to carry out her washing. She strips off completely, washes her clothes, hangs them on a hot pipe to dry and goes to sleep on the floor. This occurs in the early hours after the cleaners have finished. One of the terminal engineers, assuming the place to be empty, went to the toilet to repair something and was very shaken to discover this lady lying on the floor, whom he assumed to be dead!

There was also a man, undoubtedly mentally unstable, who when asked to move on has been known to do so whilst breaking all the fire alarm glasses on his way. This, of course, sets off the fire alarms in various places almost simultaneously, with the consequent inconvenience of evacuating buildings unnecessarily.

The trouble with all these people is that no prosecution would be successful on account of their mental state.

For some reason, some people actually come to Heathrow to attempt suicide. There was one unfortunate girl who periodically used to go to the top of Car Park 2 and threaten to throw herself off. Fortunately, the police always dissuaded her. An American, with a lot of money on him, threw himself off the Queen's Building steps. Fortunately he was not killed but, on being loaded into the ambulance, he admitted to have chosen Heathrow as the place at which he wished to depart this life!

There was another incident when I was very grateful for police assistance but, on this occasion, they did not initially wish to get involved. It was well after midnight when I received a call from the terminal staff saying that a very drunk lady was running around the check-in area claiming that her husband was trying to murder her. Our investigations revealed that she should have travelled that evening on a flight with her husband to a holiday destination. The airline on which she was to have travelled reported that the aircraft Captain had refused to take her because she would not refrain from hitting her husband. In the event, the lady was offloaded and was venting her wrath on our staff and disturbing other passengers. We asked the police for assistance but, although reluctant to get involved, they did send a WPC. The lady thus far had not committed an offence from the police point of view, but the lady then struck the WPC – fortunately she was not hurt – and the police were now involved. The Inspector arrived and, rather than have the lady in the police station overnight, he decided to put the lady on the late night bus back to London. With a sigh of relief we escorted the lady to the bus and waited for it to depart. At the last minute the door of the bus opened and the lady came out saying: "The driver tried to rape me." I was pleased to leave her with the police.

On another night, police were telephoned by a member of the public in Terminal 1 to say that some Australians were trying to steal the computer from the Aer Lingus check-in desk. Police attended and found that there was a group of Australians sleeping on some seats but the Aer Lingus computer was intact. The man who had made the call was one of the regular vagrants and the Australians were on his favourite 'bed'; he had merely wanted them removed by the police.

The incidents I have described would not normally be associated with the work of police or airport management but I included them because such happenings could take up a disproportionate amount of their time whilst also providing, on occasions, some amusement.

Before leaving the subject of the police, I must record my thanks to the Duty Inspectors and their unfailing co-operation and support. I used to meet them socially but more often when dealing with the building evacuations (for fire or security reasons), in dealing with suspicious objects, at road accidents, in crowd control situations when gurus or pop stars were passing through and, very often, at the Royal Suite.

I always enjoyed working with the airport police. One excellent Chief Superintendent at Heathrow, John Stevens, with whom I worked on security matters, has now risen to the top of his profession as the Metropolitan Police Commissioner.

Heathrow Travel Care

Heathrow was probably unique amongst airports when, in 1967, it had a welfare service provided freely to any passengers who were in difficulties. The Travellers Help unit, as it was then called, was really set up in the first place to help many foreign girls coming to this country because abortions were relatively easy to obtain in the UK. They arrived here, often frightened and unable to speak the language well, and therefore easily fell prey to people who would exploit them.

While the Travellers Help unit was there to assist passengers with problems, it became evident that the fifty thousand staff also had need for an independent counselling service. Many staff worked for small companies who did not have their own Personnel Department, and those staff who worked for large companies which did often preferred to talk their problems through with someone not connected with their company.

Thus it was that the Heathrow Counselling Service came into being. I was privileged to be its first Chairman and was ably supported by a committee comprising an airport doctor, two BOAC Personnel Managers, an airline Station Manager, the MD of the airport press, a trade union chief, a BEA Personnel Manager and a BEA accountant.

We started on the North Side in an office loaned by the BAA, and with a typewriter loaned by BOAC. The counselling was given by a qualified lady social worker called Diana Whitaker – a lovely girl who radiated Christian love without ever forcing her beliefs on anyone. Diana was very popular with staff and did an excellent job in building up the service. She later married the chaplain to the Bishop of Isfahan and was involved in an incident where she and her colleagues were being shot at in Teheran.

The Counselling Service started on day one with £25 in our account and lived rather hand-to-mouth, but we never failed to pay the staff on time. It was evident that the Heathrow Counselling Service was meeting a real need, but finance continued to be a problem.

In 1975 it became apparent that there was much to be gained from combining the Travellers Help unit and the Heathrow Counselling Service in one location and under one management – both were already registered charities. The amalgamation took place in 1975 when Heathrow Welcare was formed and was taken over for management purposes by the London Diocesan Council for Welcare.

Welcare continued the service to passengers, members of the public and staff until, in 1987, there was another change. The name of the service was changed to Heathrow Travel Care. The unit is now located in the Queen's Building and the service is ably managed by Lily Lawson, assisted by a team of qualified social workers. There is an executive committee, of which I remained a member for some years after retirement, which is primarily concerned with supporting the work and ensuring it remains financially viable.

The Service is entirely dependent on donations, and funding comes from a variety of sources including Heathrow Airport Ltd, British Airways, Hillingdon Borough, the World Health Organisation, airlines and commercial organisations operating at Heathrow. (Should there be any profit from the sale of this book I have promised that Travel Care will benefit.)

Airports (even Heathrow) can be lonely and confusing places. Every day people can find themselves thrown back on their own resources in unfamiliar surroundings and unable to cope with emotional and practical difficulties. Staff, likewise, are not immune from stress caused by problems at home or at work. Travel Care provides a professional caring service when confidentiality is assured. To quote Lily Lawson: "It would be reasonable to say that all our clients have been brought to a state of crisis by some loss which is significant to them."

The problems encountered by the service on a day-to-day basis vary enormously and range from a simple travel problem to a serious psychological breakdown.

It is hard to quantify the value of the Travel Care service to the airport and companies working on the airport because of its confidential nature. The service is of value in its own right if there was no spin-off to airport companies, but there are identifiable ways in which the service saves companies time and money.

Staff counselling has undoubtedly kept staff at work who would otherwise have reported sick, and has provided support and help for staff who may have suffered from being exposed to horrific situations. These situations are often encountered by police and fire service staff but there are also cases where airline and airport staff have to deal with relatives of those killed in a major tragedy such as the Lockerbie disaster. Other staff who helped late passengers to get on board that flight illogically felt guilty and needed help.

An example of problems passed to Travel Care: a young man arrived in Terminal 4 from South America and was booked to Germany on a flight from Terminal 1. Very late he appeared at the HAL Information Desk in Terminal 1 and said he had not travelled on the flight to Germany because he had had a premonition that the aircraft would crash. He had no luggage, which he said was against his religion. He was, however, dressed in a poncho made from a British Airways blanket stolen from his previous flight!

What the man was requesting from Heathrow airport was the rail fare to Germany. He was, needless to say, without money. Travel Care gave him a meal and the bus fare to the appropriate embassy.

There is another case of a lady who keeps coming to the airport because she says she had been told by the television to fly to Norway. She has no money for the fare and causes problems at the airline check-in desk by insisting on travelling.

Where the main tunnel emerges into the Central Area of the airport there is a large advertising sign which spans both the inbound and outbound roads. One night a man had climbed on to this sign and was threatening to throw himself down onto the traffic below. This effectively closed the airport to road traffic. His problem was, he said, that he had missed his flight to Gothenburg. He was eventually talked down, but not without causing the police, fire service and ADM (myself) much inconvenience.

After a few years at Heathrow, nothing surprises you but it was always a relief to refer these sorts of people to Travel Care.

Whilst Travel Care gives free advice and help on all subjects such as marital, financial, accommodation and phobias, including the fear of flying, it also provides a special service in the event of a major disaster. The service is automatically alerted on such occasions and provides professional support to distressed relatives (and later to staff), who are involved.

Travel Care worked tirelessly to assist the British hostages when they were released from Iraq during the Gulf War. The first such arrival received much media cover but, for many weeks thereafter, small groups of hostages would arrive, some in a very distressed state, having had to abandon their home and all possessions. On arrival they were always met by Travel Care who arranged for them to be cleared through Immigration with no delay, and then took them to a private reception area where they were given refreshments, the opportunity to meet their relations in private, and time, with help from Travel Care staff, to sort out their next move.

Through the years and under whatever title the welfare charity at Heathrow operated, it always fostered close links with surrounding Local Authority Social Services and thus, when the hostages arrived, Travel Care was able to call upon many agencies to assist them.

I will end my consideration of the excellent work of Travel Care by quoting again the unit's Manager, Lily Lawson. "We have the knowledge and the skills to offer which can make a positive contribution to airport life. We can offer not just a cup of tea, but at least a cup of tea."

Heathrow Chaplaincy – The Chapel of St. George

Shortly after I retired in 1993 I was invited to an Ecumenical Service of Thanksgiving and Celebration to mark the 25th anniversary of the founding of the Chapel at Heathrow. The service was attended by senior dignitaries of all the main churches and included Cardinal Basil Hume, the Bishop of Lambeth and the Moderator of the Free Church.

St. George's Chapel is organised on an ecumenical basis with chaplains representing Anglican, Roman Catholic and Free Church, and part-time representation from the Salvation Army. The Chapel was originally designed to have three altars, for each denomination, but I am glad to say that the spirit of unity amongst the chaplains has been so good that they all now share the same one.

The building is situated underground adjacent to the Control Tower and within easy walking distance of Terminals 1, 2 and 3. The Chapel was set up with the support and encouragement of the churches, the BAA and many of Heathrow's airlines, of which BEA and BOAC took a leading role.

The Chapel has become a heavenly haven for thousands of worshippers of all faiths, and a refuge of peace to those of no faith who want an escape from the rush of air travel. Visitors to the Chapel are constantly reminded of the Chapel's role as the church of air travellers by the plaque com-memorating the crew and passengers of Pan Am flight 103 destroyed by terrorists over Lockerbie. Also remembered is a BOAC stewardess who lost her life returning to a burning 707 to rescue passengers.

St. George's is unique in that it is underground and is designed as a vaulted crypt. A conventional church built above ground in the Central Area would have been dwarfed by the huge buildings around it. As it is, the underground construction shields the Chapel from aircraft and road traffic noise and provides an oasis of quietness and peace in the midst of a very busy airport.

At ground level, and immediately above the Chapel, is a paved courtyard with meticulously tended flower beds. In the centre of the courtyard stands a 16 foot oak cross.

The Chapel holds at least one service a day as well as being available for christenings, weddings and memorial services. Travellers and staff make up the inevitably transient congregation, and sometimes include Moslems and Jews, who regard it as a place of worship.

Apart from those who come to the Chapel to worship are those who arrive in some distress, be it separation from loved ones or fear of flying – all will find a welcome.

The chaplains have a special function in any serious emergency, can be contacted at any time by the Heathrow Operations Centre and are always advised should there be an aircraft accident.

Needless to say, the Chapel is not spared the airport vagrants who must very much stretch the patience of the chaplains, as they tend to hover around the Chapel looking for a hand-out. Some of the regulars used to attend the services to which they were welcomed, but one or two of them were very distracting to the congregation.

One little lady, who carried all her worldly goods on a Heathrow baggage trolley, was very often seen in the Chapel with her dog under her arm. The dog was taken up to the communion rails and used to growl at the chaplain as he approached. The nearer he got, the louder the barking and the congregation were all waiting to see if he would bite! One Christmas Eve the chaplains clubbed together to send this lady to an hotel for the night. When they next saw her they enquired how she enjoyed her stay. She replied that she had spent the night under the bed because the Mafia were outside her window!

Another visitor to the Chapel was a very large man who had once been a verger of a city church. He was usually drunk and would comment if he did not approve of the way in which the service was conducted. One another occasion he went to sleep and fell over backwards making a considerable noise in the middle of the service.

There was an arrangement at the airport whereby any travelling Catholic priest could obtain a key to the chapel vestry to enable him to celebrate Mass. One night the police told me they had had a complaint from a member of the public that the verger in the Chapel was very drunk. There isn't a verger, but I investigated. A visiting priest had borrowed the key, said Mass and given the key to one of the vagrants who, posing as the verger, had promised to return it. The store of communion wine was much depleted that night!

I always had a slight crisis of conscience over vagrants. In the communion service I would shake hands with them knowing that, shortly afterwards, my staff might well be ejecting them from a terminal because they were causing problems.

Speaking of 'spiritual' matters, there are many stories at Heathrow of staff encountering ghosts, but I am grateful to say I personally never met one. What I do know is that there were certain places in the airport where staff were loth to go alone at night.

One night I was called on the telephone by a supervisor in a remote building on the south side of the airport. All his staff were out on the airfield and, in spite of this, the toilet in the building had flushed and he was sure that was a ghost! He insisted someone came to ensure the ghost was removed. I volunteered and, as I expected, found nothing, but the supervisor was able to continue his duties. Prior to my visit, he was almost literally paralysed with fright.

The entrance to the underground chapel.

Heathrow Airport London

NUBIAN MAJOR

CARDOX

FOAM TENDER

WATER TENDER

RESCUE TENDER

FIRE SERVICE   APPLIANCES

A selection of Fire Service Appliances at Heathrow, about 1970.

More emergency equipment at Heathrow during the seventies:
TOP: Scammell Recovery Vehicle.
BOTTOM: Bomb Disposal Vehicle.

Two views of the Ambulance converted for water rescue (the Middlesex
County Council's sewage plant was situated close by).

Two Concordes parked at Terminal 3 before the building of Terminal 4, from where they have been operating in more recent years.

A varied selection of aircraft and vehicle items found during the 1970s on Heathrow's taxiways & runways by the Airport Ground Operations Unit

TOP: The cracked main wheel of a B.747 which shed a tyre on take-off from Runway 28R (early seventies).
BOTTOM: The tyre, which travelled to the north side of the runway and demolished a steel fence.

TOP: The author arrives to inspect the damage caused by the runaway tyre.
BOTTOM: The unfortunate car that finally stopped the tyre.

TOP: The big dig! A B.747 has its nosewheel stuck in the grass.
BOTTOM: Lifting a disabled Britannia with air bags placed under the starboard wing.

Boeing 707 G-ARWE on fire after a crash on Runway 05 on the 8th April

TOP: A Nigerian Airways DC-10 being loaded at Terminal 3.
BOTTOM: An AN-124 being loaded on Runway 23; it was too wide for the normal stands.

TOP: The flight deck of Concorde.
BOTTOM: A generation or two further on, the flight deck of a Boeing 777 makes Concorde's flight deck look old-fashioned in comparison.

CHAPTER SEVEN

TWENTY-FOUR HOURS AT
HEATHROW AIRPORT

In the previous two chapters we have looked at 'who does what' at Heathrow. We shall now briefly consider what happens on the airport on a 24-hour basis. Many people assume that the airport is dormant at night but, from the staff point of view, this is far from true. Starting at midnight, I will explain what is likely to be happening in each period of time.

Midnight–04.00

All of this period is covered by the government's night noise restrictions so, in terms of aircraft landings and take-offs, the airport is very peaceful. There may be an occasional specially approved late departure of a passenger flight, possible a VIP or Royal Flight arriving, or a medical emergency flight carrying patients, or more commonly, organs for transplant. In the case of the latter two, the aircraft type is likely to be small and quiet and will create no noise disturbance to local residents.

Although little or no flying is occurring, the airfield can be very busy. HAL takes full advantage of the night period to carry out essential maintenance on runways, taxiways and aircraft stands which are inaccessible during the day because they are in use. One runway is usually closed every night on a preplanned basis to enable this work to be carried out. Earlier in the night MASU will have completed their airfield inspection and supplied the engineers with details of all surface and lighting faults.

The airlines are busy on the stands preparing aircraft for morning departures and a great deal of surface movement of aircraft takes place between the terminal areas and the airlines' maintenance bases. Any ground-running of engines at this time is forbidden without the express permission of HAL.

MASU and ASU continue their patrols during the night, ensuring that all is safe. In particular, they check that all works areas are properly marked and lit with obstruction lights, that the stands have been correctly cleaned by MT, that the entire area in which aircraft operate is free of refuse or anything that might be sucked into a jet engine – this, of course, also applies to birds, which tend to settle on the airfield at night.

HAL uses the night period for essential cleaning and maintenance of the car parks, roads and the tunnels linking the Central Area with the outside world. If you drive to Heathrow late one night you will find two-way traffic in one bore of the tunnel because the other has been closed for cleaning. MT have a vehicle specially designed for this purpose.

Passengers are very grateful for the free provision of baggage trolleys by the airport but can have little understanding of the logistics involved in having trolleys always available at the point at which they are needed by passengers who then scatter them far and wide. A special team works through the night collecting the trolleys from all corners of the airport and restocking each trolley collection point with a predetermined number. Inevitably, many of the trolleys are abandoned by passengers in the Underground, the coach station or taxi ranks. It is a full night's work to have all the thousands of trolleys positioned ready for the morning rush.

During this period of the night, security staff and police are especially vigilant. Patrols of the airfield continue throughout, as do checks on the perimeter fence and on all parked aircraft to ensure they are locked if unattended. On the terminal forecourts, any vehicle left unattended is checked by the police and is likely to be towed away. Inside the terminals, security staff and police patrol all areas and carry out stringent scrutiny of all persons and goods entering Airside areas.

On the Airside of terminals, and particularly in the departure lounges, are numerous commercial enterprises supplying catering service or retail outlets. In recent years the number and variety of shops Airside has increased markedly and all the goods to restock the shops and bars and restaurants tend to be delivered at night. Everything has to be cleared by security staff.

In each Terminal, the Terminal Duty Officers (TDOs), of whom there may only be two on duty, are occupied checking that all terminal public areas are spotless and ready for the morning. Quite apart from any other consideration, this involves walking miles checking all the remote gaterooms (the passenger travelators are switched off at night).

Another task for the TDOs during this period is to check the correct operation of lift alarms, security alarms and fire alarms for their Terminal. All the alarms should alert the TDO in the Terminal Control Centre and have to be individually tested to ensure that they do so (otherwise some unfortunate person might spend the night stuck in a car park lift).

In general, TDOs who encounter a passenger problem at the beginning of this period are likely to be with it till the morning. It is in this context that I cannot praise too highly the kindness shown by TDOs to passengers in difficulties. There are many cases, I am sure, that are never known about, but I have known many instances of TDOs giving their rest room to mothers with children, buying food for people with no money and going out of their way to help well beyond the requirements of their job description.

On one night an Asian mother was due to travel with a very young infant but, at the last minute, refused to enter the aircraft through fear. She spoke no English and was found in a distressed state by one of the TDOs. It was by now after midnight, so the lady TDO made the mother comfortable in her own rest room and arranged food for her. A serious problem then became apparent. She would neither feed, change nor even hold the baby, who was obviously hungry. The TDO, who was fortunately an experienced mother, managed to acquire the necessary to bottle, feed and change the infant. She cared for the two all night, found someone amongst the cleaning staff who spoke the mother's language and was eventually able to contact relations of the mother in Birmingham. The TDO stayed with the mother in her own time until the relations arrived.

By this period of the night, the 'resident vagrants' who have avoided being moved on have settled down for the night on the airport in their chosen spot and are no problem. One little lady usually sleeps in the passport photo booth in the corridor linking Terminals 1 and 2. I normally avoided talking to this lady as she would subject anyone who spoke to her with a torrent of abuse. A lady colleague of mine was soundly rebuked by the same lady for wasting her money (the little lady's) on redecorating the corridor! Another 'gentleman of the road' locks himself in the Chapel toilet and is easily detected through the snores coming forth therefrom.

The Heathrow Operations Centre (HOC) is busy throughout the night doing not only its own work but that of the terminal information desks whose telephones are all switched through to HOC at night. Calls are received throughout the night which are mainly requests for flight information or for information about trains and buses (of which there are few at night), but calls also come from people such as the lonely, insomniacs, the suicidal and party-goers who have over-indulged.

One lady from America kept ringing HOC saying that the CIA in London had stolen her passport. She would not believe our staff when they said they, regrettably, could do little to help. She kept calling and eventually the telephone exchange had to contact their colleagues in America to stop these calls which were monopolising staff time and important telephone lines.

Apart from the above, staff in HOC are keeping a watch on the ever-changing ETAs (estimated arrival times) of the early flights and planning the allocation of aircraft stands for the day ahead. At all times, of course, HOC fulfills its main purpose of being the airport's operational nerve centre ready to react to any incident or emergency.

04.00–08.00

For staff who have worked through the night, this is a period when they have to change the airport from a cleaning, checking and maintenance mode to one of peak activity.

On the airfield this is one of the most beautiful times of the day with the early flights from the Far East or the Gulf landing as dawn breaks. MASU will have been busy inspecting the runway before the first flight lands and ensuring it is clear of birds and anything that could be hazardous to aircraft. In the summer months one runway is kept out of service in the early morning for what is called a 'walking inspection.' A walking inspection involves Operations and Engineering staff walking the length of and carrying out a detailed inspection of the entire runway (12,800 ft), and every light fitting on the runway has to be cleaned. These lights are required to have a minimum intensity but, due to aircraft operation, become covered in a film of dirt which has to be removed. This is done by subjecting them to a blast of ground-up walnut shells. After cleaning, the light output of the lights is checked.

During the walking inspection all the white paint markings are renewed as these, like the lights, become obscured by aircraft operations. The centreline and touchdown zone markings become badly blackened by rubber deposited by aircraft tyres. The paint dries very quickly and, at the end of the walking inspection, it is handed back to ATC by MASU as fit for immediate use.

During the winter these walking inspections take place in the afternoon because of the lack of light in the early morning.

From around 05.30 there is a great build-up of road traffic into the airport, much of it bringing in staff for the morning shifts. The consumption of electricity at this time must reflect the number of electric kettles being switched on for that 'cuppa.' One thing essential to the efficient working of shift staff is tea, especially the first one of the day.

The terminals start the period polished, scrubbed and empty with all the trolleys neatly stacked and the check-in desks all restocked with labels, boarding passes, etc.

The shops and catering outlets open up and take inside supplies of such things as newspapers and milk delivered and left outside their door overnight. Escalators and travelators are switched on, any faults having been rectified during the night. In the Baggage Reclaim Hall, HAL staff will be preallocating baggage reclaim units to arriving flights in accordance with the ETAs displayed on the VDU in front of them in the Control Room. The airlines are responsible for delivering the baggage from arriving flights onto a belt outside the Arrivals building, as allocated by HAL. From then on, HAL is responsible for delivering the baggage to passengers on the Reclaim Unit as displayed on the screens in the Arrivals Hall.

Apart from the reawakening seen in the Terminals, there is a steady increase in public transport as taxis, buses and long-distance coaches flood into the Central Area – the London Underground system also returns to operation. The Queen's Building Medical Centre reopens at 06.00 and all the security control posts guarding the airside areas are manned up ready for the busy period ahead. As the aircraft movements start there is a huge build-up of vehicles and people needing to gain access to airside through the control posts. All will need to be scrupulously checked and problems can be encountered with incorrectly documented vehicles or people wishing to meet VIP flights. Such vehicles are held in a layby until sorted out in order to prevent a blockage at the control post. Other early-morning vehicles needing to go to airside will be aircraft cleaning and catering trucks, Post Office lorries, refuelling vehicles, crew coaches and even the milk float.

The VIP lounges will have been in use any time from 04.30 because of early arriving flights in Terminals 3 and 4 from The Gulf or the Far East. Flights are not scheduled to arrive that early but favourable winds on a flight direct from Hong Kong, for example, can greatly reduce the scheduled flight time. Well before the arrival of a flight carrying a VIP, the meeters and greeters will have arrived at the suite. Before 05.30, the ADM may well be coping alone with two geographically separated VIP suites simultaneously until he gratefully hands over to the early shift Special Facilities Officers when they arrive bright and cheerful at 05.30.

During this period (04.00–08.00) UK airports are particularly susceptible to radiation fog after long clear nights and can often involve Heathrow in receiving arriving flights from other airports which are fogbound. On these occasions, arrangements have to be made to look after the passengers until representatives of the airline in question can get to Heathrow. In some cases, the diverting airlines already have a handling agreement with a Heathrow-based airline, which makes life much easier. On occasions of mass diversions to Heathrow parking space for aircraft becomes a problem and at times Runway 23 has to be used for this purpose.

On some occasions, of course, Heathrow, is itself afflicted by fog, which will cause delays and cancellations to aircraft not equipped for CAT 3 operations. When fog conditions prevail, every effort is made to make delayed passengers as comfortable as possible. For example, terminal staff increase greatly the supply of seats, and catering outlets are enhanced.

However dense the fog at Heathrow, aircraft operations will continue by CAT 3 aircraft and this will require constant patrols by ASU and MASU to ensure that no vehicles on the airfield stray into restricted areas. In the Control Tower, ATC will be watching all ground movements on the ASMI screen and will be passing regular updates on RVRs (runway visual range) to incoming pilots as they themselves receive new figures from the Transmissometers alongside the runways. These RVRs will also be supplied automatically on VDUs to airline offices to assist them in planning their operations.

08.00–16.00

This period of the day at Heathrow used to consist of peaks and troughs, but now the airport is operating so near maximum capacity that there are few troughs and aircraft 'slots' are in great demand. From a commercial point of view there is an ideal time for any airline to operate its service to a given destination. When more than one airline is operating to that destination, each will wish to have the same commercially-ideal time. This is obviously impossible, and therefore negotiations must take place to establish who operates when. If you multiply this problem by the number of airlines at Heathrow and compound the problem with the fact that there are few spare slots, you will understand that an independent arbitrator is needed to sort it all out.

There used to be a Scheduling Committee whose task it was to sort out the varying requirements of the airlines in terms of schedules, with impartiality. The task is now undertaken by Airport Co-ordination Ltd., who process all applications for aircraft arrivals and departures. The task is to maximise the use of the airport, satisfy the commercial needs of the airlines and to ensure that operations are so planned and operated that they do not conflict with government regulations in respect of noise.

It will be obvious from the above that there is not much space available in this period for general aviation aircraft. These are, in the main, private and executive aircraft and, although ATC and the Operations Duty Managers do all they can to facilitate them, they still take second place to scheduled airline operations.

The terminals are all steadily busy during this period, each having its own particular peaks of activity, dependent on the schedules of its resident airlines. Terminals 1 and 2, which are used mainly for shorthaul flights within Europe, are busy early (06.00 onwards) in departures and relatively quiet in arrivals, whereas Terminals 3 and 4, which mainly serve long haul intercontinental airlines, are very busy in arrivals any time from 04.30 and yet quiet in departures.

Many of the passengers passing through Heathrow are transfer passengers who are only using the airport as a connecting point at which to change from one flight to another in order to reach their final destination. There are basically two types of transfer passenger: the intercontinental/-international passengers who remain airside at all times and never technically land in the UK and the international/domestic passengers transferring between internal UK flights and international ones. These passengers transfer landside. The advent of the EEC has slightly complicated these arrangements.

Transfer passenger traffic is of enormous financial value to airlines and to Heathrow. In the early days of Atlantic crossings by aircraft, their limited range and position of the Great Circle track from New York or Montreal to Europe made London and Prestwick geographically the natural Atlantic gateways at which passengers from North America would change to flights to Europe, Africa, Asia and Australasia.

The great improvement in aircraft range and performance means that Heathrow now has to compete on equal terms with airports like Paris, Amsterdam and Frankfurt for its share of the transfer passenger market. Because of this, Heathrow is going to great lengths to ensure its service to transfer passengers is better than that provided by other airports and has recently invested a lot of money in a specially-designed Transfer building to provide every comfort and convenience to the passengers.

Whilst on the subject of transfer passengers, Heathrow never assumes they have been adequately security-screened at the point of embarkation and always re-searches them prior to their boarding a flight from Heathrow.

These searches reveal some unlikely things. One passenger was found to be clutching a large spider in his hand which he claimed to be his best friend and without whom he never travelled! On another occasion a duffel bag was being X-rayed when the security staff noticed something unusual. Stuffed into the bottom of the bag, and almost dead, were four tiny monkeys. The animals were handed over to the RSPCA in the Airport Animal Quarantine station, and in time recovered; they were being smuggled from South America to a European customer.

Apart from having to search all transfer passengers arriving from other terminals, each terminal has to search all its own departing passengers, and the number of staff required for this obviously depends on the number of passengers booked on any one day by the airlines. HAL supplies staff to cover the task in accordance with passenger estimates supplied by the airlines, and normally this works well. Occasionally passengers exceed the estimates and the staff allocated are too few. This would result in queues and inconvenience to passengers. Should such a situation look likely, the ADM will arrange to transfer staff from another terminal to help out until the peak is over. The accurate matching of staff numbers to the task at any one time is one of the great challenges faced by airport managers. However good one's preplanning has been, some aircraft will fail to operate to their correct schedules for all sorts of reasons, such as technical failure or destination weather. This can create unforeseen peaks in a terminal's operations.

As has already been explained, Heathrow is operating to capacity during this period and is therefore very vulnerable to a major disruption however caused. Heathrow operates like a well-oiled machine when passengers and aircraft flow in and out unimpeded but, should anything obstruct this flow, congestion can occur very rapidly, not only in the terminals but also on the roads and in the car parks.

The causes of major disruption to the smooth operation of the airport are usually well beyond the control of its management. If, for example, the ATC computer at West Drayton fails, as all computers do at times, staff in ATC have to revert to the old manual methods which will considerably reduce aircraft movements with the resultant build-up of a backlog of flights.

More common than the above and more aggravating because they are deliberate are the industrial disputes which seem to take place almost annually affecting French, Spanish or Greek Air Traffic Control services. For Heathrow, flights problems with the French ATC are obviously the most difficult to cope with because of the large numbers of east- and south-bound flights routed through French airspace. Every effort is made to re-flightplan to avoid the areas affected by industrial action, but there is a limit to the extra air traffic neighbouring countries are willing or able to handle.

In addition to industrial action, some airspace suddenly becomes unusable because of the outbreak of hostilities, as in the recent case of Yugoslavia. In the case of the Gulf War, there was so little notice of the start of hostilities that a British Airways aircraft, its crew and passengers were trapped at Kuwait airport.

Nearer to home, serious disruption can arise when it becomes necessary, for some reason, to evacuate one or, very rarely, all of the terminal buildings. HAL is very safety conscious and will err on the side of caution every time there appears to be some danger to the occupants of a building.

One day, when Terminal 4 was very busy, I received a message from the police that seven British Airways workers in the baggage sorting area of the building had been affected by poisoned fumes and taken to hospital. The building was evacuated whilst we awaited the arrival of the Surrey Fire Brigade, who are responsible for the south side of Heathrow. The problem was thought most likely to have come from the spillage of a volatile chemical, so the firemen donned their appropriate gear, resembling spacesuits. A long time passed – or what seemed a long time – but the firemen found nothing. There was no smell nor any obvious spillage but firemen, being cautious by nature, would not let people re-enter the building, so I was making plans to transfer flights to other terminals. This is not something one undertakes lightly, particularly in the case of Terminal 4 which is geographically remote from the other terminals and this can result in great confusion to 'meeters and greeters,' not to mention airline staff.

Fortunately, before flight transfers to other terminals became unavoidable, the cause of the problem was found. A very large cardboard box (part of somebody's baggage) had fallen off a conveyor and burst open near the intake of the ventilation system. The box had contained nothing but rather potent curry powder, which had been sucked into the ventilation system and delivered in a concentrated dose to the unfortunate British Airways staff! Soon after the discovery of the cause, passengers and staff were readmitted to the terminal, but the delays caused by this incident affected the terminal for hours after.

Something else that requires careful management on busy days is car park capacity. As explained in an earlier chapter, different car parks are provided to suit all needs and pockets, but inevitably there are times when demand for one particular type of park may exceed the supply. Obviously a passenger intent on catching a flight cannot be turned away, so when a particular car park looks in danger of being full, diversion arrangements are immediately introduced – the customer usually gains by getting a higher-rated car park.

During a busy day the terminal concourses and terminal staff are constantly on the watch for people who should not be there and may be causing congestion. In this category they would place unauthorised film crews from the media, people collecting money or promoting some product and even people holding in impromptu concert. I once found a man on a terminal forecourt who had erected a blackboard and was giving a lecture!

I don't wish to give the impression that HAL is against the press or collecting for charities, but these things must be prearranged to avoid problems. HAL has, in fact, an excellent relationship with the media which it goes to great lengths to foster.

16.00–20.00

If ever there is to be a slight lull in the feverish activity in the terminals it will probably occur during the early part of this period. Towards 20.00 there is a great increase in activity in the shorthaul Terminals 1 and 2 which coincides with the end of a business day and this increase is particularly marked on Friday nights in Terminal 1. At this time, the road traffic on the terminal forecourt has to be carefully controlled by HAL staff and police to prevent serious congestion.

It is during this period that the office and day staff depart and, before they do, they hand over to the operational staff any information or anticipated problems for the coming night. These might be urgent engineering work on the airfield, VIPs, new carpets to be laid in the terminal, a new advertising display to be erected or a new terminal gate-room to be opened.

The Operations Duty Manager will be finalising plans for work to be carried out on the airfield overnight or on the following day. He will complete a 'Works Permit' for each task and write on the permit the safety conditions which must be complied with by those carrying out the work. The completed permits are then distributed to Air Traffic Control and to MASU, who will ensure the safety conditions are adhered to.

Before starting work on the airfield each day the supervisor will contact ATC for final clearance to start. This is necessary because, since the permit was issued, conditions may have changed. For example, the wind may be different from that forecast requiring the use of a different runway pattern which, in turn, means that the piece of concrete the engineers were to have isolated for work is now essential for ground movement of aircraft to and from the runway.

The working relations between ATC and HAL are such that these problems are resolved amicably. It is more difficult when ready-mix concrete has already arrived for repairing a part of the airfield which ATC now find they must keep in use.

One afternoon I was advised, via radio, that a lady passenger going to Nairobi on a British Airways flight had collapsed in Terminal 4 and had been taken by ambulance to the nearby Ashford Hospital. This was not, in itself, unusual; with over 50 million (in the year 2000 this has risen to 62 million) passengers passing through the airport annually, medical emergencies are not uncommon, but the same lady reappeared at the terminal within half an hour looking perfectly healthy and checked in for the flight.

I later received another message that the Captain of this same flight was refusing to depart until a certain passenger was taken off the aircraft. The passenger turned out to be the one who had been taken to hospital. Once strapped into her seat on the aircraft, she had called the stewardess and said she might 'blow up' the aircraft. She was duly removed from the aircraft and brought back to landside. Her baggage had to be retrieved from the aircraft hold, which with a B.747 takes some time. The lady appeared to have ample money and elected to stay in an hotel overnight so she was put in a taxi. She then jumped out of the taxi and disappeared into the terminal again and was eventually traced in a toilet where she was happily sitting in the 'lotus position.'

The unfortunate lady was handed over to the Social Services but I mentioned the incident to prove that whenever you are looking forward with joyful anticipation to a quieter period in the day, something invariably happens to spoil it. This one lady had caused HAL staff, airline staff and fellow passengers a great deal of trouble.

20.00–24.00

This is possibly the most challenging period of the day. There is a deadline of 23.30 by which all the day's aircraft operations must be completed (apart from exceptions previously mentioned). Terminals 3 and 4 have many longhaul departures to Africa, the Far East, US and Australia and, amongst all these, it is not unusual for one or more of these aircraft to suffer technical troubles. Most of these aircraft are B.747s with large passenger loads. If the problem is not resolved, an overnight stop is involved. All the passengers have to return their Duty Free purchases and pass back through Immigration to Arrivals. From there, they are taken to hotels. Most airlines look after their passengers very well on these occasions but there are exceptions. In these cases, a heavy burden falls on the Terminal Duty Officer to ensure the passengers, particularly women and children, are cared for.

Fortunately, technical delays on modern aircraft do not last too long. I well remember a rather difficult week in India back in about 1957 when I had to share a hotel with a full passenger-load of a BOAC Britannia bound for London; the aircraft had been beset with a series of faults and was delayed for six days. As a matter of interest, this Britannia carried the registration G-ANBG, which was changed to G-APLL in March 1958 for reasons which are perhaps not too difficult to understand! Being the representative of the airline I used to be regaled with the various versions of "BOAC," such as "Be 'Ome At Christmas" and "Better On A Camel"!

Particular problems are experienced by terminal staff when transit flights, or those diverted to Heathrow, are forced to stop overnight and contain certain passengers who are not permitted to land in the UK. An example is a Russian flight operating Moscow–Shannon–Cuba which diverts to Heathrow because of bad weather in Shannon. Immigration might well refuse to allow such passengers to landside.

Terminal 1 remains busy up to 23.30 with flights scheduled to operate late in the evening to such places as Israel, Ireland and Cyprus. Terminal 1 also has to cope with late flights which should have operated through Terminal 2 but are sufficiently behind schedule to necessitate their being transferred. Terminal 2 does not normally handle flights after 23.00 and is not staffed to do so.

Whilst terminal and airline staff are busy getting the last flights away, they can be beset with the strangest of people who seem drawn to Heathrow at night! One night I was called to Terminal 2 where a very smartly dressed African man was walking up and down the concourse throwing down £10 notes as he went. Initially our staff had picked them up and given them back. Communication was difficult because the man had a 'walkman' radio on his head. I eventually pulled aside one earpiece and asked what he was up to. The man then took a passport out of his pocket and said: "I am a diplomat – you can't touch me." The diplomatic passport was not out of his pocket long enough for me to examine it so, after he became aggressive, I called the police. They were also given the diplomatic story but they eventually managed to grab the document, which turned out to be a book on owls! Very soon the man and police left the terminal together.

The staff in Terminal 1 called me after 23.00 one night because they had a difficult lady who insisted that they telephone Edward Heath, the former Prime Minister, and ask him to come and collect her. On arrival in the terminal, I was introduced to a formidable elderly lady who would have done justice to the part of Lady Bracknell in 'The Importance of being Ernest." Her story was that she was a relation of President Reagan and that she and Edward Heath were flying next day to a Reagan family gathering in America. We asked if there were any others from England joining the party and were told that one such was Father O'Reagan from Bristol. A check on the telephone revealed that there was a priest there of that name. The story seemed more and more plausible but by now it was after midnight and I was very loathe to disturb Mr Heath.

Fortunately the 'handbag' came to the rescue. An observant member of our staff noted a label on the lady's bag with a phone number in Belfast. We called the number and spoke to a lady, who said: "Mother is always doing this sort of thing – please send her back in the morning"! At least Mr Heath was undisturbed that night.

As the airport passengers disappear from the terminals, the airport enters its cleaning and maintenance phase. Teams of cleaners swoop on the floor areas vacated by passengers and staff and sweep and polish them to appear as new. Terminal staff are reduced to the minimum consistent with security and efficiency. Terminal engineering staff take advantage of the night period to service all the lifts, travelators, baggage belts and reclaim units and for installing new equipment.

On the airfield operations side, the ODM will be on the alert for any aircraft attempting to breach the night noise regulations. This, in reality, can be quite complicated as the regulations are so designed that conditions vary from one aircraft type to another and also from one aircraft to another of the same type which may have slightly different engines. Thus, each individual aircraft must be checked to establish exactly what restrictions apply to it.

On the airfield, MASU will be doing their checks of airfield lighting asking ATC to bring up the routes of green lights as necessary. They will also be checking that all works areas and obstructions are safe and properly lit with red lights – temporary works areas are lit with 'Glim lights' placed there by ASU.

Engineers will have cleared with ATC and started the night's work on the taxiways and runways, one of which is usually closed overnight for maintenance.

On the airport, road diversions will be in evidence where resurfacing work is in progress and very often one bore of the main tunnel is closed for cleaning. This time of night is also chosen for moving into or out of the Central Area vehicles carrying large items of plant or equipment such as cranes or portable buildings.

As the night proceeds, Security staff remain vigilant and HOC prepares for the morning and looks after the public who won't go to bed!

CHAPTER EIGHT

EMERGENCIES AND PAN AMERICAN 103 (LOCKERBIE)

Heathrow as an airport has an excellent safety record which is due, in the main, to the extensive preparation and planning undertaken to ensure that this is so. Safety and security has always been the top priority of all the airport's objectives.

The emergencies for which the airport must be prepared fall broadly into four categories – building fires, medical, terrorist action (real or threatened, to which all forms of public buildings and transport undertakings are now susceptible) and aircraft-related emergencies.

To deal first with domestic fires. Every public building is 'fire certificated' and all HAL staff are trained by the airport Fire Service in the use of fire extinguishers, building evacuation, fire assembly points and all aspects of ensuring the safety of life. This training is both theoretical and practical, staff being required to use extinguishers on real fires and to carry out building evacuations.

Because Heathrow has its own fire service, response to any fire call is very rapid and this response is always backed up by the Local Authority fire service. Because of the vigilance of airport staff, any fires that do occur are rapidly dealt with and serious fire damage is very rare.

If one is unfortunate to suffer a heart attack or other serious illness in a public place, Heathrow is probably one of the best places in which to do so in terms of the prompt assistance available. In all areas of the airport there are staff with radios who can, via their control centres, summon an ambulance immediately. Many staff are trained in First Aid and all terminals have readily available defibrillator and intubation kits which can be taken very rapidly to the patient to be used by any medically qualified person.

Doctors and nurses are available from various medical centres both in the Central Area and on the south side of the airport. I have already described the HAL Medical Centre in the Queen's Building and there is, in the same building, a British Airways Medical Centre. In addition to these, there are medical staff employed by 'Port Health' whose main function is health screening of immigrants, but they are always ready to help in an emergency.

Thus, whatever illness may strike, much skilled help is available on site and the London Ambulance Service (LAS), which has an ambulance station on the north side of the airport, can be called very quickly.

In this age, all transport is liable to be used by terrorists in pursuit of their cause and, of course, air transport is no exception. However, because air transport was one of the earliest forms of transport to suffer terrorist attention, it is now the best able to deal with it. I obviously cannot give any details of the security measures taken by Heathrow, but suffice it to say that Heathrow's expertise in this field is recognised by many foreign airport managements and Heathrow staff are sent to train their staff. Heathrow security staff also train staff of other transport undertakings in the UK. Heathrow Airport Security leads the world.

I shall deal in more detail with aircraft-related accidents as it is with these that airport emergency services are usually associated. Serious aircraft accidents always receive immense media coverage but they are, in reality, extremely rare. During 35 years at Heathrow, I experienced only four such accidents which, when considered in the context of a daily aircraft movement of well over 1,000, is a very small number. I would add that in each of these accidents, the cause was in the aircraft itself and in no way related to the airport or its facilities.

Because of the rarity of aircraft accidents, every year Heathrow is required by the CAA to simulate a major aircraft accident. This exercise involves all the airport's own emergency services and all the outside services that would be called out if the accident were real. For the exercise a real aircraft is usually filled with staff volunteers who represent the passengers and some are made up most realistically by the London Ambulance Service to show what injuries they have sustained – this is not a sight for the squeamish! There is also usually a real fire to extinguish.

The purpose of the exercise is primarily to ensure that the Heathrow Emergency Orders, published by Heathrow Airport Ltd., which list in detail all the functions of the emergency services (on and off the airport), operate well in practice, and to enable all participating services to refresh their memory of them. After all such exercises, all participating services meet to discuss the exercise and to find means of improving still further, Heathrow's ability to deal rapidly and efficiently with any incident – the overall priority being always to **save life**.

It may well be of interest to readers to know how a serious accident would be dealt with at Heathrow. As part of the requirements for maintaining its licence to operate as an airport, Heathrow is required to publish the Emergency Orders, already referred to. From the pushing by ATC of the CRASH alarm, every emergency service and all airport staff will act in accordance with these orders. When an accident has occurred, there is no time for briefing and familiarity by all with the orders is therefore vital – hence the annual exercise.

I will, therefore, take a hypothetical accident and show what action each organisation would play. Let us assume that an aircraft has called ATC saying that it has a serious engine fire with smoke in the cabin and is returning to Heathrow for an emergency landing.

ATC staff would immediately use the CRASH alarm which would alert the airport Fire Service.

Immediately following the CRASH alarm would come a message giving the emergency a priority category, details of the aircraft, its ETA, the runway to be used and its passenger numbers etc. Also given will be the Rendezvous Point (RVP) for the assembly of off-airport emergency services. In this case, the emergency category would be 'Aircraft Accident Imminent' which, together with 'Aircraft Accident' is the highest priority. ATC will only use 'Aircraft Accident Imminent' when it is almost inevitably going to develop into an 'Aircraft Accident.'

For lesser emergencies, there are other priorities such as 'Full Emergency' or 'Local Standby.' Depending on the emergency category given by ATC a different level of attendance will be provided by the emergency services. Obviously in the case we are considering, the maximum attendance would be provided.

Let us assume that the aircraft, having landed heavily, has come to a halt at the mid-point of the runway and become engulfed in flame. ATC would issue an 'Upgrade Aircraft Accident Imminent to Aircraft Accident' message, this time adding the airfield block number in which the aircraft is located.

Airport Fire Service

Because of the previous 'Aircraft Accident Imminent' message the airport Fire Service vehicles would already be deployed alongside the runway and would surround the aircraft immediately it stopped. The first priority would be to suppress the flames with the very powerful foam jets to facilitate the safe evacuation of people and to allow access by Fire Service personnel into the aircraft to assist with any injured. The aim is to remove all the aircraft's occupants to a place of safety clear of the aircraft before attention is given to saving the aircraft itself.

The airport's own fire appliances have a great capacity for delivering extinguishing foam very rapidly but, with a prolonged operation, additional water (a constituent part of the foam) will be needed. This can come from the Fire main, a high pressure hydrant system which covers the whole airfield, or from the London Fire Brigade appliances which would, by this time, be on site.

The airport Fire Service, on receipt of the 'Accident' message from ATC, immediately alerts the London Fire Brigade Headquarters and the London Ambulance Service Headquarters and passes to them essential details and, in particular, the Emergency Service Rendezvous Point at Heathrow at which they should assemble. The Rendezvous Points are specially designed assembly areas for emergency vehicles from which they can be led rapidly to the site of the accident. All Rendezvous Points are equipped with a telephone and have easy access to the airfield. Heathrow used to have six Rendezvous Points, but the present four is found to be adequate. Quite logically, these are RVPs North, South, East and West. Formerly there were also RVPs North-West and South-East.

After all passengers and crew have been removed to a place of safety, the Fire Services will ensure that all fires are out and the aircraft is safe before handing it over to the police who will guard it until the arrival of the Air Accident Investigation Branch (AAIB). The police ensure that no evidence which might be of value to the AAIB is tampered with.

Airport Telephone Exchange

The airport telephone exchange is staffed by HAL personnel and plays a very important part in emergencies. All emergency calls from ATC to the AFS are monitored and recorded by the exchange which, in turn, is responsible for advising all relevant airport organisations details of the ATC emergency message.

Metropolitan Police

The police constantly monitor the ATC emergency line and have a statutory duty to take charge of an accident. Therefore the first airport policeman, of whatever rank, to reach the accident scene becomes the Police Incident Officer and will establish an incident post. Initially this will be his car, but this will be replaced with the purpose-built Incident Vehicle, a mobile office with all the necessary communications facilities. A senior officer will soon arrive and assume command of the scene.

The AFS will already be in action carrying out immediate rescue operations and will advise the Police Incident Officer of any assistance required from outside fire services which will have assembled at the designated RVP. At the RVP will be a police unit, probably a motorcycle patrol, who will assume the duty of RVP Officer and send forward, from the RVP to the accident site, any emergency services as requested via radio by the Incident Officer. Because these outside services do not carry the Heathrow ATC radio frequencies and may not be familiar with the airfield geography, they must be led to the accident by Marshalling ("Follow Me") vehicles provided by the ASU.

At the accident site, all the attending emergency services set up their own incident control vehicles from which each senior officer (LFB and LAS) controls the activities of his own service in compliance with the overall command of the Police Incident Officer.

Direct to the scene MT will deliver the Emergency Medical vehicle, together with three inflatable hospital tents, each with its own lighting. These tents will be erected in a position dictated by the Police Incident Officer – normally upwind of the accident site and easily accessible by LAS ambulances which do not have cross-country capability.

The Police Incident Officer remains in charge of the scene until all persons have been rescued and removed from the site. He will be responsible for all passenger property left on the site and for its ultimate return to its owner. He is responsible for excluding all unauthorised persons from the site and for handing the aircraft over to the AAIB.

Away from the accident scene the police have other duties. In the police station, a 'Major Incident and Casualty Bureau' is established. The bureau will remain in operation until all passengers and crew have been accounted for. At Heathrow this is usually done in co-operation with the British Airways EPIC Centre (Emergency Passenger Information Centre) which offers its services to all airlines. EPIC will supply the police with passenger details and, very importantly, details of any hazardous cargo on the aircraft which might endanger rescue services. The sorting and returning of property to its rightful owner is also undertaken by the police station.

After the rescued passengers have been sorted according to their immediate medical needs, they will be taken to the Emergency Reception Centre (ERC) in the airport buildings – if unhurt – or to hospital. Wherever they are sent, a member of the police will go.

Police also attend the Incident Information Bureau (IIB), the place where relatives and friends are cared for until reunited with their passenger.

In the case of a very serious accident the police will set up and staff a temporary mortuary.

The London Fire Brigade (LFB)

On receipt of the emergency call from the AFS, the LFB will dispatch fire appliances immediately to the RVP given and will report on arrival to the police RVP officer. These appliances will then be led to the accident site by ASU and will provide back-up to the AFS in fire-fighting and rescue. The LFB vehicles have first priority at the RVP and are sent forward without delay.

The LFB also alerts other Local Authority fire services as necessary. The south side of the airport, for example, falls within the area of responsibility of the Surrey Fire Brigade.

London Ambulance Service (LAS)

On receipt of the emergency message, the LAS will dispatch ambulances immediately to the RVP given in the message. It always alerts the designated hospitals to stand by for casualties and to dispatch surgical teams, if necessary. The designated hospitals for Heathrow are Hillingdon, Ashford and West Middlesex.

St. John's Ambulance Brigade is advised by the LAS of the accident and usually it attends and assists in the Emergency Reception Centre.

On arrival at the RVP, the LAS ambulances report to the RVP Officer and are led to the accident scene when called for by the Police Incident Officer. They will park near the inflatable hospital tents and immediately take the most urgent cases to hospital. The medical staff on site will have established 'Triage,' the examining of accident victims and sorting them according to medical priority.

Hal Queen's Building Medical Centre

When an accident has occurred a MASU vehicle collects staff from the Medical Centre and takes them directly to the accident site where the inflatable tents are being erected. They will give First Aid and start the Triage process. They will initially be few in number, but soon they will be assisted by LAS staff and other medical staff summoned for the emergency, including the specialist surgical team sent from the designated hospitals.

Operations Duty Manager And Staff

The Operations Duty Manager would usually go to the accident site and assist the Police Incident Officer, who often needs the ODM's intimate knowledge of the airfield and of the HAL organisation.

The ODM is, as always, responsible for the safety of aircraft operations and he must decide to what extent flights can continue when part of the airfield is rendered unusable by the stricken aircraft and the fire and rescue vehicles going to and from it.

Heathrow is fortunate in having three runways and can therefore usually maintain a reduced service in the immediate aftermath of the accident and return to full operations as soon as all obstructions are cleared from the airfield.

As already explained, MASU staff take the HAL medical staff to the accident and will thereafter ensure that the area of the accident is isolated from those parts of the airfield still in use by aircraft. Access to the accident area will be closed off with cones and red lights. MASU will be responsible, finally, for inspecting the accident area after the aircraft has been removed and handing it back to ATC as safe for use.

ASU will dispatch leader vehicles to the RVP and escort outside emergency service vehicles to the accident as directed by the RVP Officer. It will arrange for the airline or handling agent of the accident aircraft to assemble on an aircraft stand ground equipment such as passenger coaches, aircraft steps and baggage-loading vehicles. Once assembled, they are ready to be led to the aircraft when called for by the Police Incident Officer.

Throughout the emergency operation, the ASU will be fully committed in leading vehicles to and from the accident site.

The ODM will agree with the AAIB when the aircraft can be moved clear of the airfield and will arrange with the airline how this is to be done. If necessary, HAL MT can assist with salvage equipment and expertise. The ODM is naturally keen to return Heathrow to being fully operational as quickly as possible.

Under the control of the Operations Duty Officer is the MT section and, as already explained, their first responsibility when an accident has occurred is to position the Medical Emergency Vehicle to the accident site and thereafter to erect the inflatable hospital tents. The MT unit then stands by to provide specialist equipment such as heavy lifting gear and mobile lighting. When the emergency is over, MT staff are often involved in the removal of any wreckage. They are trained in salvage methods and aim to remove any aircraft speedily without causing it any further damage.

Terminals

When an accident occurs all terminals become involved, whether or not the aircraft concerned operates from that terminal.

The Information Desk staff in all terminals need to be aware of the facts and must be told what information is to be given to enquirers. The ADM will decide what is to be told to general enquirers, but any relatives and friends meeting passengers on the accident aircraft will be directed to the Incident Information Bureau (IIB) in the Queen's Building which will have been opened and staffed by Terminal 2. People will be guided to the IIB by HAL staff posted along the route from the respective terminals.

The location now set aside for use as the IIB is the British Airways Executive Club in Terminal 1 which is most comfortable and ideal for the purpose. Unfortunately, should the lounge be needed as the IIB, the Executive Club passengers have to be asked to leave .

Terminal 1 will automatically set up and supply staff for the Emergency Reception Centre (ERC) in the Eurolounge, if necessary repositioning flights using the lounge to other gaterooms.

All terminals will have staff made available to act as stretcher bearers should they be called for by the Police Incident Officer. Coaches will be on standby to deliver them to the accident site.

Should the accident curtail aircraft operations in and out of Heathrow, even for a short period, this can cause delays and congestion in the public areas and consideration has to be given to providing additional seating and catering.

Hal Engineering

On being advised of the accident, the Airport Duty Engineering Manager will go to the scene and advise the Police Incident Officer whether there are in the area any electrical services which would be a hazard to the emergency services, and isolate them as necessary. He will also assess what damage has been done to the airfield and its equipment so that rapid repairs can be carried out as soon as the emergency phase is over.

Airlines

British Airways has an Emergency Passenger Information Centre (EPIC) in the Queen's Building which it makes available to any airline whose aircraft has been involved in an accident. The telephone number of EPIC is given to the media and thence to the public. One function of EPIC is to provide a service to the public, to record and deal with all enquiries, to establish beyond doubt who was on the aircraft and where they have been sent, ie, to the ERC or to hospital. Although neither the Lockerbie nor the East Midlands disaster was near Heathrow, EPIC was set up for both these accidents and proved invaluable.

EPIC, of course, also works very closely with the police, who have the ultimate responsibility for establishing who was on board and what happened to them.

Aside from the function of EPIC, there is an onus on the airline whose aircraft is involved in an accident to advise the AFS of the number of passengers, crew and animals on board, together with details of any hazardous cargo.

The airline must also despatch ground equipment such as steps and coaches to the assembly point given them by ASU. When required, they will be led to the accident site. The coaches will take uninjured survivors to the ERC.

Airline staff will be sent to the ERC, IIB and to the police Major Incident Room in the police station.

Heathrow Operations Centre

HOC provides an all-important co-ordinating role in ensuring that the emergency activities are proceeding correctly and in keeping an accurate log of all happenings. HOC will call in any necessary staff who may not be on the airport. This includes senior airport management, an off-duty ADM to assist the police, airport Chaplains, Travel Care staff and, most importantly, Public Affairs staff.

The role of the PA staff is to deal with the press and TV reporters who will descend *en masse* on Heathrow looking for information. Every assistance is given to them by our PA staff, who keep them well informed whilst preventing them from getting in the way of those directly involved in dealing with the emergency. The media can be of great assistance in passing information from the airport management to the public. Such advice will often cover details of road congestion around Heathrow and whether prospective passengers should come to the airport or not.

One of the byproducts of an aircraft accident is the large number of voyeurs who rush to the scene, sometimes seriously impeding the emergency services. This was the case when the Trident crashed near the Crooked Billet roundabout in Staines.

Obviously, the vital need after an emergency is to get any injured to hospital without delay. Should there ever be any problem in evacuating patients by road, arrangements are already prepared to use RAF helicopters and, should very large numbers be involved, to use the London Underground trains in an ambulance role.

After the rescue phase of an accident has been completed, the main priority is for the airport to care for the passengers in the ERC and their relatives and friends in the IIB and to reunite them as soon as possible. To care for them are HAL terminal staff, airline staff, police, chaplains and the professional counselling staff from Travel Care.

In summary, Heathrow is extremely well prepared and equipped to handle any disaster. Pilots have great faith in Heathrow's Emergency Services and in its ATC and safety standards.

PAN AMERICAN FLIGHT 103 – LOCKERBIE
(Appendix to Chapter 8)

This appalling disaster caused by terrorist activity has been well documented, but now those thought to be responsible are being brought to trial, I thought it might be of interest to readers to see how Heathrow reacted on that night.

I had just arrived in my office at Heathrow at 19.50 on the 21st December 1988 to take over from my day ADM colleague when news started coming through the media of an aircraft accident. Staff in HOC had seen a news flash on TV Channel 4.

Checks with ATC revealed that this aircraft was Pan Am Flight 103 which had been scheduled to depart Heathrow at 18.00 and had actually become airborne at 18.25. We later learned that Scottish ATC had initiated an alert at 19.18 when radio contact was lost. My colleague stayed on for a while to act as a liaison link with Pan Am while I found myself restricted to the office and HOC because of the arrangements that needed to be made and because of the flood of inbound calls from media and the public.

Although the accident was not on Heathrow, EPIC was set up by British Airways and I told Terminal 2 to set up the IIB. This was particularly difficult on this evening because the accommodation then earmarked for use as the IIB had been set up for a pre-Christmas staff sale and was therefore stacked with all manner of sale goods on display. Our Terminal 2 staff excelled themselves and the IIB was fully operational one hour before the first relative arrived.

Staff available in the IIB by 21.00 were HAL staff, Pan Am staff, police and two chaplains. By this time, EPIC and the Police Major Incident Room were also in operation.

All appropriate senior staff were advised and the Public Affairs staff arrived at the airport and were in action very quickly. I was able to tell the telephone exchange by 20.40 that all press calls could be put through to Public Affairs. For the public, the telephone numbers had already been given to the media, who had published them widely on radio and television.

At 23.00 Pan Am arranged to cancel their morning B.727 flight to Germany and use it to take their senior management and the AAIB to Carlisle. The Hillingdon suite was opened up at 23.30 for the departure of the US Ambassador and his party by a special C-130 aircraft to Carlisle.

Apart from the above, there were eight other extra flights arranged for the press, taking them to Edinburgh or Carlisle.

At 23.30 I met up with the Principal Security Adviser of the Department of Transport, who is responsible for security standards at all UK airports. At this stage the cause of the disaster had not been attributed to a bomb.

By 02.45, 39 enquirers had been looked after by the IIB staff but, unfortunately, it was not till around 05.00 that the Scottish Police released any firm information. There are few things more stressful for staff than not being able to give information to people who are desperately worried, and this sort of strain can tell months later. Travel Care provided special help for staff suffering in this way.

Before first light, I arranged for all flags on the airport to be lowered to half mast.

Heathrow staff, without exception, had worked superbly through the night and, in particular, to care for distressed relatives. Many staff volunteered to stay on duty whilst those at home called in offering their help. Co-operation between HAL staff, ATC, Pan Am and the police was excellent.

Many of the Heathrow police were sent to Lockerbie to assist at the accident site, a very difficult and unpleasant task at which they performed admirably.

I will quote the Pan American's Director commenting on that night: "I realised that the airport was a close-knit community, but not to this extent. Heathrow responded magnificently and people came in or phoned with offers of help."

The BAA Managing Director, Airports Division, wrote a note to the Heathrow Airport Director saying: "I felt very proud of the Heathrow team when I read the ADM report for 21/22 Dec. Please pass on to them my sincere thanks for a job well done."

Pan Am 103, its crew and passengers will never be forgotten by Heathrow and a memorial plaque is in the chapel for all to see. It is very sad, however, that Pan Am is no longer one of the Heathrow airlines. I have happy memories of my dealings with Pan Am staff on Northside Heathrow, Terminal 3 and many foreign airports.

CHAPTER NINE

THE FUTURE

The Members of the anti-aviation lobby, and particularly the minority referred to in the Introduction who wish Heathrow did not exist, would appreciate a *"Daily Express"* cartoon from a 1979 edition of that newspaper.

The picture depicts a guide speaking to some Arab tourists. The guide is standing beside a sign which says "National Trust. Historic ruins of Heathrow Airport." In the background are the main exhibits, Ye Olde Terminal 3 and Ye Olde Control Tower. The guide is saying to the Arab tourists: "Before your fathers wisely made oil too expensive to buy, this place was hell on earth where millions of people were herded together . . .

For those who know and understand Heathrow, it is inconceivable that this airport will ever cease to be a world leader. Heathrow has grown and prospered since, on the 1st January 1946, the Air Ministry (RAF) handed the aerodrome over to the Civil Aviation Authorities and will, I am sure, continue to do so.

In the years since I retired from Heathrow, many new developments are evident. The crosswind runway 23/05 has been moved south-eastwards to give more space for expansion in the Central Area, and the High Speed Rail Link and the new Transfer Terminal are now completed and in operation. This is evidence, if it were needed, that Heathrow has prepared itself for a healthy and prosperous future in which the service given to passengers and customer airlines will always be a priority.

The most exciting project in the immediate future is, of course, Terminal 5, to be built at the west end of the airport between the main runways.

Since retiring I have continued my aviation association by endeavouring to teach Air Training Corps cadets (1349 Woking Squadron) to fly a Link Trainer. I also maintain my PPL, flying mainly at Fairoaks. I have for several years been involved with a beautiful DH Dove 8, G-ARHW, which is based at Fairoaks and was displayed in a three-ship formation with two other Doves in the 1998 Farnborough Air Display.

It is through this association that this book came to be published. In 1999 we took the Dove to the Great Vintage Flying Weekend at Kemble, where I met the organiser, Peter Campbell, whom I had not seen since we were both prep-school boys. Peter, who is also a book publisher, rashly expressed an interest in publishing my ramblings. They would otherwise have for ever gathered dust – so thank you, Peter!

I cannot finish this book without saying how grateful I am to have worked at Heathrow, both with the airlines and with the Airport Operator – BAA/Heathrow Airport Ltd. Almost without exception I have been amongst very pleasant colleagues and I have found around the world that those associated with aviation are easy to live alongside. Maybe we all suffer from this strange addiction of liking to work near aeroplanes

I close with sincere thanks to BOAC, BEA and BAA for enabling me to get to know and appreciate Heathrow, and I repeat the title of the book:

"VIVAT HEATHROW!" – "long live Heathrow!"